Opera 33
Guide

Maria Jeritza as Jenůfa. She was the first to sing the role in America, at the Metropolitan Opera, New York, in 1924 (photo: Metropolitan Opera Archives)

Preface

This series, published under the auspices of English National Opera and The Royal Opera, aims to prepare audiences to evaluate and enjoy opera performances. Each book contains the complete text, set out in the original language together with a current performing translation. The accompanying essays have been commissioned as general introductions to aspects of interest in each work. As many illustrations and musical examples as possible have been included because the sound and spectacle of opera are clearly central to any sympathetic appreciation of it. We hope that, as companions to the opera should be, they are well-informed, witty and attractive.

Nicholas John
Series Editor

33

Jenůfa / Katya Kabanova

Leoš Janáček

Opera Guide Series Editor: Nicholas John

WITHDRAWI

Published in association with
English National Opera and The Royal Opera

John Calder · London
Riverrun Press · New York

First published in Great Britain, 1985 by
John Calder (Publishers) Ltd.,
18 Brewer Street,
London W1R 4AS

First published in the U.S.A., 1985 by
Riverrun Press Inc.,
1170 Broadway,
New York, NY 10001

BRITISH LIBRARY CATALOGUING IN PUBLICATION DATA

Janáček, Leoš
    Jenůfa (*Katya Kabanova*). — (Opera guide; 33)
    1. Operas — Librettos
    I. Title   II. Preissova, Gabriela   III. Kraus, Otakar   IV. Downes, Edward
    O.D.   V. Tucker, Norman, *1910-78*
    VI. Janáček, Leoš Katya Kabanova   VII. English National Opera   VIII Royal
    Opera   IX. Series
    782.1′2   ML410.J18

ISBN 0-7145-4081-1

Typeset in Plantin by Margaret Spooner Typesetting, Bridport, Dorset
Printed by Camelot Press Ltd, Southampton

Contents

List of Illustrations

Picture research: Henrietta Bredin

A National Composer

Jaroslav Krejči

Janáček, a man of sensitive mind and passionate temper, was born in the north-eastern corner of the Czech geographical area (the historical lands of Bohemia, Moravia and parts of Silesia). The year was 1854, and the Czechs had re-emerged from obscurity as a nation, becoming increasingly conscious of their national identity.

Janáček's work was largely inspired by folk music and topics from Czech history or the history of other Slavic nations. The folkloristic inspiration came primarily from his native Moravia, or rather its eastern part, where the folksongs displayed a more lyrical, emotional and variegated formation. It took some time before Janáček's style found its way to the hearts of the sophisticated, rather traditionally-minded milieu of the Czech capital, Prague (in Bohemia). But once this happened, the gate was open to the musical world at large. Significantly this was at the time of World War I, as a result of which the Czechs emancipated themselves from Austrian domination and entered the world arena on an equal footing with other nations.

To understand why the nationality issue dominated the social landscape so much in Janáček's time, a few words have to be said on earlier historical developments.

As a result of the Thirty Years' War (1618-1648) the Czechs lost their predominantly Protestant aristocracy and cultural elite, and their lands (lands of the Bohemian Crown which bore the title of St Wenceslas) were subsequently incorporated bit by bit into the hereditary domains of the Austrian Habsburgs. It was a period when, amongst the Czechs, music and visual art flourished above the level of folklore, but literature did not, and political representation of the Czechs as a nation was virtually non-existent.

At the turn of the eighteenth and nineteenth centuries the dual impact of the Enlightenment and of Romanticism prompted a revival of the Czech literary language. The Enlightenment favoured rational solutions; this meant tolerance and pluralism in religious matters, but uniformity and standardisation in the state administration and language. Thus the Austrian Habsburgs began to enforce the German language as the language of their domains. The Romantics on the other hand defended the right of each individual nation to assert its own linguistic and cultural identity. Thus, the Czechs' resentment of government pressure was strengthened by scholarly arguments in favour of their own language. The result was a cultural revival which, in due course, was followed by political aspirations.

The geographical area of the Czech nation, *i.e.* the historical lands of Bohemia, Moravia and parts of Silesia, was surrounded on three sides (north, west and south) by German speakers, and in the three lands themselves there lived many ethnic Germans (at that time more than a third of the total population). In the mixed areas and wherever there were suitable conditions for it, there was a tendency on the part of the authorities to extend the usage of the German language. This found expression in the education policy. Though the schools were in principle state-run, the Czech schools had often to be financed by private means. There was a continuous tug-of-war for schools and children. The German employers (most of the nascent industry was owned by Germans) were often instrumental in that policy.

Though Janáček was born in a wholly Czech village, it was not far from the ethnic border. Most of his life was spent in the Moravian capital Brno, which in those days was dominated by its fiercely nationalistic German minority, a situation which could not but lead to confrontation and which necessarily made an impact on him.

Janáček's lifespan coincided with an epoch of manifold tensions and complex and rapid social change. In his youth, he experienced the frustrating failure of the Czech aspiration to transform the multi-ethnic Habsburg Empire into a federation, with a more representative government. The first step, the introduction of a constitutional parliamentary regime (1861) seemed promising, but within six years it became clear that the Emperor (Franz Josef I) and the ruling German-speaking Austrian elite were ready to make serious concessions only to one particular nation, namely the Hungarians. In 1867 the Habsburg Empire became the dual Austro-Hungarian monarchy. The demands of the Czechs and of other Slavic nations in the Empire remained unheeded. These nations were giving up the hope that the Empire could be transformed into a genuine fatherland for all its nationalities.

Thus the Slavic feelings flared up again. They found manifest expression for the first time in 1848, when the German nationalist liberals campaigned for the convocation of a pan-German parliament in Frankfurt, in which all the lands of the Habsburg Empire should have been represented. The Slavs in the Austrian domains, however, rejected this invitation, and instead called their Slavic congress in Prague in the same year.

After the Austro-Hungarian deal the disappointed Czech politicians and intellectuals decided to turn for help to the Slavs outside the Empire. Russia as the most powerful Slavic nation was the obvious choice. This mood found its demonstrative expression in the 'national pilgrimage' of the Czechs to the ethnographic exhibition in Moscow in 1867.

Janáček was then 13 and a pupil of the German Grammar School in Brno. Two years later he switched to the Czech Teachers' College in the same city. His Slavic, especially pro-Russian, feelings matured only in 1896, when he visited St Petersburg where his brother Francis lived. A series of enthusiastic feuilletons which Janáček then published in a Brno newspaper, bears witness to the deep impression this Slavic imperial city made on him. A year later in Brno he founded, together with other enthusiasts, the Russian Circle, of which he later (in 1909) became Chairman.

In spite of his love for Russia Janáček also had good Polish friends. He showed a keen interest in Polish music and visited Poland five times, usually on the way to or from Russia. On one of these visits, in 1904, he almost became director of the Warsaw Conservatoire, but a misunderstanding with the Russian governor frustrated this.

Meanwhile, further changes took place in his country which fuelled the Czechs' drive for emancipation. Rapid industrialisation created a large working class which soon found its political representation in the Social Democratic Party. In principle this party should have been internationally minded, which would have weakened the centrifugal tendencies of the non-German, mainly Slavic, nationalities. In 1878, however, the Czechs founded their own Social Democratic Party which later, in 1891, put into its programme the demand for the transformation of the Austro-Hungarian monarchy into a federation on ethnic lines. There was no significant movement amongst the Czechs which would condone the centralising tendencies within each part of the Dual Monarchy.

The British premiere of 'Katya Kabanova' at Sadler's Wells in 1951; producer, Dennis Arundell; scenery, Anson-Glass; costumes, Anthony Boyes. Kate Jackson (behind) as Kabanicha, John Kentish as Tichon and Amy Shuard as Katya (photo: Angus McBean© Harvard Theatre Collection)

In fact the policy of successive Austrian governments oscillated between the two positions: small concessions or no concessions. Once some concessions were made, the German nationalists protested or even rioted and their deputies in the Bohemian diet (the lands were endowed with a limited autonomy) abstained. If the government took a tough line, it was the Czech deputies who abstained from the parliament in Vienna. On the whole, the government muddled through.

In 1905 the situation became dramatic on several counts. The dominant issue was the fight for universal, equal suffrage. Demonstrations took place on both sides of the ethnic divide. The agitation culminated in a one-day general strike all over the country. The common action of the non-enfranchised population seemed to have taken some of the steam out of the ethnic rivalries. Furthermore, the compromise between the Czech and German representatives in Moravia (the so-called Moravian Pact) on the basis of mutual concessions, a compromise approved by the Moravian diet and sanctioned by the Emperor, offered the prospect of a more peaceful coexistence of the two nationalities in that particular land.

Nevertheless the Moravian capital Brno became the scene of violent clashes between the participants in a German rally from all parts of Austria on the one hand, and on the other hand, the Czechs demonstrating on behalf of the foundation of a Czech University in Brno, which would have been the second Czech University. (The Charles University in Prague had, in 1881, been divided into two universities, one Czech and one German.) The Army was called in to restore order and one young Czech worker was shot dead. Janáček reacted in his special way; he composed a sonata for piano, to which he gave the title: *First October 1905 — From the Street*.

Meanwhile, Janáček became more aware of the interconnected tissue of social and ethno-linguistic problems. As amongst the employers there were many more Germans than Czechs and, on the other hand, the Czechs were over-represented amongst the workers, industrial confrontation often coincided with the contest between the two nations. This was especially the case in the eastern, highly industrialised, part of Silesia, where the many coal mines and steel mills were almost exclusively German property and where the local Slavic population was partly Czech and partly Polish. It was a region not far from Janáček's birthplace (about six miles as the crow flies). The people there spoke the same Lachian dialect as Janáček's ancestors and it was not too difficult for them to accommodate themselves to the Polish language if necessary. Though in principle both the Czechs and the Poles in that area were subject to the same Germanising pressure, nevertheless there was some competition between these two Slavic nations, to the great distress of the pan-Slavists.

Janáček turned his attention to the two-fold social-cum-linguistic issue in composing men's choruses to the words of three songs by the Czech Silesian poet Petr Bezruč. One called *Maryčka Magdonova* is the story of a poor orphan girl who, in charge of her five younger brothers and sisters, commits suicide because of her merciless environment; the other, *Schoolmaster Halfar*, is a tragedy of a Czech teacher who does not want to give up teaching in his mother tongue; and the third, *Seventy Thousand*, refers to the number to which the Czech speakers in eastern Silesia were reduced as a result of German pressure and Polish competition.

The great test of anybody's nationalism came during the World War 1914-1918. The Czechs as Austrian citizens had to fight on the Austrian side; their sympathies were, however, largely with the opposite side, to which in many instances they eagerly surrendered. Janáček, because of his correspondence with Russian friends and with a leading Croatian politician, was classified as 'politically suspicious' by the Austrian police. In 1915 his Russian Circle in Brno was banned, and one of its members jailed.

In the same year Janáček began to compose his orchestral rhapsody *Taras Bulba*, based on a novel by N.V. Gogol. The theme was the heroic and tragic struggle of the Cossacks in the 17th century against Polish rule in the Ukraine — a topic not too encouraging for a Slavic heart. In fact, it reflected the contemporary situation. In World War I, until mid-1917, a legion of Polish volunteers fought against the Russians on the side of the Austrians, from whom the Poles then expected more understanding for the reconstitution of the Polish State than from the Russians. On the other hand, the Czech liberation movement abroad (headed by Professor T.G. Masaryk and joined by the Slovak representatives) organised, from the ranks of Austrian prisoners of war, the Czechoslovak legions who fought on the side of the Russians, French and Italians.

In 1916 the National Theatre in Prague, after years of opposition, eventually staged *Jenůfa*, and its première proved to be a tremendous success. As a result, Janáček made the acquaintance of a prominent critic and writer, the Prague German Max Brod who, by translating the libretto into German, helped him to win international recognition.

At the beginning of 1918 Janáček's *Jenůfa*, in Brod's translation, was scheduled for the Court Theatre in Vienna. Janáček's main concern was to safeguard, in the German language performances, the national character of the opera. But the danger lay elsewhere. As the plan to stage the opera became known, a group of German nationalist deputies in the Parliament in Vienna raised objections, claiming that at a time when the Czech soldiers betrayed the Empire by going over to the enemy, it would be improper to perform a Czech nationalist opera on the official stage in the capital. A Czech nationalist newspaper in Prague immediately — as a quid pro quo — suggested the barring of German operettas from theatres in Prague. Janáček was trapped in the nationalist crossfire. Himself an ardent nationalist, who in Brno would not attend a German theatre (Brno was for him a kind of battlefield in his own country), Janáček was happy at the prospect of seeing his opera performed on the Imperial stage in Vienna (as it were, 'abroad'). A Viennese production was all the more attractive because the Czech National Theatre in Prague had not put it on until 1916, twelve years after the première in Brno. So, Janáček complained to the editor of the Prague newspaper that operettas (lower-grade music in his view) should not be taken as a bargaining point against his opera. The final decision was made, however, at the top level. It was the new Emperor, Charles I (installed in November 1916) who, stricken by the misfortunes on the battlefield, embarked on a more conciliatory policy towards his non-German subjects. *Jenůfa* was played on his personal order and Janáček scored a triumphant success.

Yet Janáček did not escape a nationalist reprimand from the Czech side. A young art critic, Zdeněk Nejedlý, found it 'bizarre' that, in allowing his opera to be played in a German theatre, Janáček did not preserve his national honour. Having denounced the Viennese performance of *Jenůfa* as a 'pasquinade', and 'a disgrace', Nejedlý recalled the example of Bedřich Smetana who, on the occasion of the performance of his *Two Widows* in Hamburg, protested against the transposition of the scene to France, and allegedly did not want his music to be played abroad any more, as it was destined for his countrymen and not for glory abroad. Most people, however, would find this stance rather bizarre. It may be added as a piquant reminder that Professor Nejedlý, as a dedicated Communist, became, after the Communist takeover in Czechoslovakia in 1948, Minister of Education and eventually President of the Czechoslovak Academy of Sciences. He died in 1962.

Eight months after *Jenůfa* won the day in the Viennese Court Theatre, the Czechs seceded from Austria and the Slovaks from Hungary. On October 28, 1918, the Czechoslovak Republic was born. Also as a result of the war, the Poles emancipated themselves from their three masters, between whom they were divided, *viz*. Russia, Germany and Austria. The Serbs, Croats and Slovenes created a common state which was later called Yugoslavia. All these Slavic nations were triumphant. Of the Slavs only the Bulgarians who had fought on the German side suffered territorial losses, and the Ukranians, whose western territories became a part of Poland, had to be satisfied with a federated status within the USSR. The Russians who, after the revolution, accepted the principle of national self-determination, had to see (temporarily, as we now know) several nations secede from their empire.

In 1919 Janáček resumed his function as Chairman of the renewed Russian Circle in Brno. He served in that capacity until 1921. Meanwhile his beloved Russia underwent fundamental changes. The newly created Czechoslovakia offered a refuge for thousands of Russian and Ukrainian exiles. The pro-Slavic feelings took another turn.

After the war, in free Czechoslovakia, Janáček composed two operas inspired by Realist classics of Russian literature, *Katya Kabanova* and *From the House of the Dead*, and two others based on Czech librettos (*The Cunning Little Vixen* and *The Makropulos Case*). He also reworked his first opera *Šarka*, on a Czech national myth. A Slavic topic *par excellence* was the cantata, *The Glagolitic Mass* (Glagolitsa is the oldest Slavonic script, devised by St Cyril, while what is known as the cyrillic script, was the work of the pupils of his brother St Methodius).

In 1925 Janáček was granted an honorary Ph.D. degree at the newly founded Czech University — the Masaryk University in Brno. He very much treasured this honour. In 1927 he was nominated a member of the Prussian Academy of Arts in Berlin. This was, perhaps, the ultimate recognition he received from the German public. As many other foreign awards and invitations show, his music did not remain confined to home consumption. His many tours abroad, amongst them one to England (in 1926), contributed to his fame.

Janáček's last-but-one musical creation, composed in the year of his death (1928), was a men's chorus on the occasion of the laying of the foundation stone for the building of Masaryk University in Brno. The death of a young worker on October 1, 1905 was vindicated. Janáček immortalised both the martyr and the victory in his musical bequest.

Drama into Libretto

Karel Brusak

'The theme of the play, which reeks of the criminal courts, is elaborated in complete accordance with the recipe already provided by Tolstoy, Strindberg and Hauptmann, and its basic idea, the murder of a baby, is particularly reminiscent of Tolstoy's *The Power of Darkness*. The good points of the play are weighed down by the unsympathetic and embarrassing atmosphere of the whole, which suggests the pen of a young literary rebel rather than that of a woman.'[1] This opinion, expressed by the leading Czech poet Jaroslav Vrchlický (1853-1912) after the first night at the Prague National Theatre of the drama which several years later Janáček used for the libretto of his opera, was not exceptional. The play *Her Step-Daughter* (*Jeji pastorkyňa*) by the twenty-eight-year-old Gabriela Preissová (1862-1946), which was produced for the first time on November 9, 1890, and published a few weeks later, caused a commotion among the critics as well as the public, and initiated a furious controversy between the advocates of realism in art and their opponents. The attitude of most of the critics was negative. 'The play tried to be naturalistic but became brutal; it tried to be truthful but became repulsive because art was pushed aside.'[2] 'Everything in it is covered by the frost of baseness, vulgarity, foolishness and contemptibility.'[3] 'One part of the play should properly be set in a foundling asylum, the second in a maternity hospital and the third in a prison.'[4] Several critics castigated Preissová for insulting the pious and moral peasants of Moravian Slovakia by depicting them as immoral and even criminal. On the other hand several young critics, and particularly those Slovak ones who knew the village society portrayed by Preissová, praised both the veracity and the dramatic strength of the play. But even though the opponents of the play were in the majority and even though the director of the National Theatre Fr. A. Šubert (1849-1915) wrote a letter to an important Prague daily soon after the first night claiming rather defensively that 'it would be a fatal mistake if the National Theatre were to close its doors to new movements and particularly to such a healthy and legitimate movement as realism in art',[5] both the production of Preissová's drama and the subsequent discussion around it helped to establish the style of Critical Realism in Czech drama.

Several Czech dramatists had attemped from the late 'eighties onwards to portray typical Czech life as truthfully as possible. Following the Russians Belinski and Dobrolyubov rather than the Western theoreticians of Realism, they had taken their subject matter from the village as they were convinced that it was only there that typical Czech life could be found. This was the time of the exploration of village life, its folklore and its music, in the study of which Janáček took a prominent part, culminating in the Ethnographical

1 *Hlas národa*, November 11, 1890.

2 Jan Ladecký (1861-1907), dramatist and critic, in *Česká Thalia*, November 20, 1890.

3 Josef Turnovský (1838-1901), writer and critic, in *Zábavné listy*, 1890, no. 4.

4 Josef Kiři Kolár (1812-1896), actor and dramatist, as quoted in a letter by A. Sluková to T. Nováková, November 17, 1890.

5 *Národní listy*, December 7, 1890.

Exhibition in Prague in 1895. But even when dealing with the darker side of village life — the bigotry, greed, brutality and alcoholism — Czech dramatists of this period had always avoided naturalism and hardly ever saw their characters as being influenced by social conditions. They were Romantics as far as the structure of the drama and psychology of the characters were concerned and Realists only in the setting, local colour, details and dialogue. Preissová went further in her first play *The Farmer's Woman* (*Gazdina roba*), a dramatisation of her own short story. The play was produced at the Prague National Theatre a year before *Her Step-Daughter* and although much closer to Realism than her later play it earned almost general acclaim. The reason was that the critics misunderstood it. They saw it as a conventional drama of adultery reminiscent of *Le Maître de forges* by Georges Ohnet (1848-1918), with the difference that Preissová had transposed the story to a lower social milieu of villagers from Moravian Slovakia and given it a tragic ending. Apart from Shakespeare and classical tragedies, the plays of Ohnet, together with those of Victorien Sardou (1831-1908), and Eugène Scribe (1791-1861), constituted the principal fare of the National Theatre. Contemporary realist, naturalist, psychological and symbolist plays were almost completely neglected even though they had been translated and published in the review *Česka Thalia* and could be seen in both the German theatres in Prague.

Preissová's *Her Step-Daughter* came, in a way, much closer to Romanticism than her first play due to the ballad-like subject: the tale of a seduced girl set in a secluded mill and a lonely cottage. Romanticism was also apparent in the parallelism between the mood and nature — the sunset in the first act, the windy moonlit night in the second, the frosty winter day in the third. As in the case of *The Farmer's Woman* the plot was based on actual events of which Preissová heard during a stay in Moravian Slovakia. One was the crime of a jealous peasant who deliberately slashed the face of his brother's fiancée with whom he himself was in love. The second crime was that of a woman who helped her step-daughter to kill her illegitimate baby. Preissová used the first without changing it but altered the second because, as she wrote later, she wanted to create two contrasting female characters.[6] Jenůfa, the step-daughter in the play, was too gentle to be a murderess and the deed had to be committed by the step-mother alone.

Preissová's drama can be interpreted at several levels. Primarily it can be seen as a drama of four main characters: the Kostelnička, her step-daughter Jenůfa, Jenůfa's lover Števa and his step-brother Laca. The real heroine is the step-mother, the Kostelnička. This is already implied by the pronoun 'her' in the title which indicates the Kostelnička's possessiveness. She is a woman of great will and strict moral principles, an exception amongst the backward villagers. She is trusted by the priest who has put her in charge of the chapel; hence her nickname the Kostelnička, the 'Sacristan', derived from the Czech 'kostel', church. She leads religious processions, takes care of burials and she also knows how to cure the sick. She understands the force of love because she is the widow of a man whom she married for love who became a drunkard, squandered their money and beat her. When he dies, she is left destitute with Jenůfa, his daughter from his first marriage. But she is not crushed. Peddling victuals from the village to the town she makes enough money to support both herself and Jenůfa; the girl becomes the centre of her life. Preissová said many years later that she wanted to show 'a barren woman haunted with a painful

6 In a letter to *Pražske večerni noviny*, November 30, 1890.

Lorna Haywood (above) in the title role and (below) Sylvia Fisher as Kabanicha and Dennis Wicks as Dikoy in 'Katya Kabanova' at ENO (photos: Donald Southern)

desire for a child'.[7] The Kostelnička is proud that she surpasses all natural mothers by sacrificing herself for her step-daughter, whom she has brought up to be better than all the other girls in the village and for whom she has prepared a sumptuous dowry. When a woman remarks that only a natural mother can truly feel for her child, the Kostelnička observes defiantly that every cat knows how to be a mother even if she has no kittens of her own. After Laca, the step-brother of Jenůfa's lover Števa, slashes Jenůfa's face out of jealousy, and after Števa ceases to love Jenůfa who is already pregnant by him, pride makes the Kostelnička fear that people will brand Jenůfa as a fallen woman and blame her for having brought her up the wrong way. She conceals the birth of the child, humbles herself before Števa to try to make him marry Jenůfa and, when she does not succeed puts her hope in Laca. When he refuses to take Jenůfa with Števa's child, the Kostelnička on impulse tells him that the child has died. Although this was an unconscious reaction, she has to endure its consequences. Her murder of the baby becomes inevitable. From what we know of the Kostelnička this is not in keeping with her character and it introduces an element of determinism which is foreign to the rest of the play. Preissová obviously did not want to create the impression that Kostelnička's crime was premeditated but, as she had to motivate it somehow, she makes the Kostelnička rationalise her fortuitous decision. In a monologue the Kostelnička rejects outright the idea of giving the child away, because Jenůfa would not allow it; she argues that drowning will be quicker than possible death from diphtheria, and consoles herself with the idea that the child's death will save an adult life and preserve both Jenůfa's honour and her own; she further maintains that the child is the fruit of sin. But, at the same time, the Kostelnička is shown to be mentally deranged and unable to appreciate the seriousness of her action. Janáček tried to correct this flaw in the play by playing down the Kostelnička's rationalisation of the murder and by stressing her momentary insanity.

The second main character, Jenůfa, appears at the beginning as rather passive and colourless. She is too good to be true. She is the prettiest girl in the village, charming and sensible. She is the best singer; she has taught a shepherd boy to read and a servant girl to embroider. But she is so blinded by love that she does not want to realise that Števa is a shallow braggard and philanderer even when it becomes obvious that he does not love her. Only at the end of the play is she raised from her passivity: she persuades Laca to make friends with Števa, and she shows a determination to create a new life for herself. Even if she seems to be aware that her life with Laca will be full of strife her consent to marriage seems sudden. Preissová later realised that this was a rather facile solution and, in her second version of the play published in 1912, she made considerable changes in the final scene. Jenůfa admits that she will never forget her sacrificed child and only agrees to marry Laca when he promises that he will share her suffering. These additions strengthened the ethical idea of the drama.

The realism of the play is most apparent in the almost incidental portrayal of village society. There is a strict dividing line between the poor peasants and the rich farmers. Števa, a rich miller, is not recruited for the army but his poor step-brother Laca has to spend three years in the service. Like any other man of his social standing Števa tries to rid himself of the reponsibility for his illegitimate child by offering money on condition that nobody will be told that he is the father. The Kostelnička's friend, the poor and sick widow of a

7 *Svoboda*, January 16, 1941.

Elisabeth Söderström as Katya Kabanova and Jeffrey Lawton as Tichon. Welsh National Opera, 1982; producer, David Pountney; designer, Maria Björnson (photo: Julian Sheppard)

17

shepherd, prays to live for at least two years more until her two boys finish their apprenticeship. There is alcoholism, bigotry, superstition and envy. Everybody knows about everybody else. For this reason it is highly improbable that the Kostelnička could have concealed the pregnant Jenůfa in her cottage for five months pretending that she had gone to Vienna. The undisputed master of the village is the mayor, who is always on good terms with the higher authorities. After jilting Jenůfa, Števa is accepted by him as a suitable match for his neither too clever nor pretty daughter Karolka. But the social criticism is probably unintentional. In the revised version, Preissová omitted Laca's outburst against social injustice, and changed the figure of the poor widow into the widow of a farmer to make her socially more suitable to be the Kostelnička's friend.

The view that the play is a drama of ideas is perhaps closer to Preissová's intention. Her most original contribution was her feminist approach to the characters. Both the Kostelnička and Jenůfa are, in spite of their shortcomings, superior to the male characters. They will rise again from their humiliation because Preissová believes that one can atone for any crime through penance and that God's mercy is boundless. As Jenůfa says: 'I shall prove to you that I shall rise above my guilt. Neither should my step-mother be cursed by you. Don't condemn her, give her time to repent.' When, forty years later, Preissová reworked the play into a novella, she ended it with Kostelnička's release from prison. She dies peacefully at the house of Laca and Jenůfa, and the only shadow over her last days is her regret that she will not live to see the birth of their child.

At the time when the campaign for Realism was being waged in Prague, Brno — where Janáček worked as a teacher of music at the Teachers' Training College and as Director of the Organ School — was a backwater of Czech culture, two-thirds of its inhabitants being German. Janáček took little interest in the intellectual life of distant Prague and it seems that he became acquainted with Preissová's drama only in 1892 when it was produced in Brno. He was always interested in themes of tragic eroticism. In 1887 he wrote *Šarka*, based on the neo-romantic dramatic poem by Julius Zeyer (1841-1901), inspired by its heroine whose passionate hatred changes to passionate love. He was similarly attracted by the themes of destructive love, jealousy and guilt in Preissová's drama, by its setting in Moravian Slovakia and its folkloric elements, and perhaps also because it offered him the opportunity to be the first Czech composer to use prose instead of verse for an opera libretto. In the case of *Šarka*, Janáček failed to obtain permission for the use of his own libretto from Zeyer (who was only approached after the score was finished). On the other hand Preissová, who shared Janáček's interest in folk music, was only too pleased with his plan to turn her drama into an opera. He began working both on the libretto and on the score in 1894, and it took him seven years to complete the opera.

Janáček's libretto retains the structure of the play in which each act ends with a moment of high drama — Laca's slashing of Jenůfa's face with a knife in the first act, Kostelnička's killing of the baby in the second act, and her confession in the third. The fate of each character remains the same; the repentant Kostelnička goes to prison, Jenůfa and Laca look towards a new life and Števa is rejected by Karolka. But Janáček made several changes in order to increase the dramatic tension and suit his musical intentions.

Important among these changes was the addition of songs composed by him to folk verse. Preissová, unlike other Czech dramatists, used folk music very sparingly. There are only two folk songs in her play. The first, which the drunken Števa orders the four fiddlers to play because it is Jenůfa's favourite song, is in fact neither played nor sing as the Kostelnička stops the fiddlers before they can begin. Here Janáček included a lengthy song which is so daringly erotic that it seems highly improbable that it could have been Jenůfa's favourite. This is followed by a wild dance which likewise does not occur in Preissová's drama. In addition, Janáček included the song of the recruits and a quartet with a chorus which repeats many times over that every couple has troubles which they must overcome. This piece of trite folk wisdom is an attempt to minimise the deepening conflict between Števa and Jenůfa and it is rather incongruous that Laca should take part in the quartet. The second song included by Preissová, which is sung by three girls at the gathering in the Kostelnička's cottage before Jenůfa's wedding with Laca, was left unchanged. These additions give the libretto a much stronger folk flavour than that of the drama, to which Preissová did not object and, with the exception of the dance, she included them in the later editions of her play.

No less substantial were the cuts in the dialogue. In the first Act Janáček shortened the dialogue between the Kostelnička and the wife of the mayor of the village. This speeded up the pace but left out an important element of the drama, namely the fact that all the main characters are related. Jenůfa is Števa's cousin and Laca's step-cousin; the old mother Buryja who lives with them in the mill is Jenůfa's and Števa's grandmother, and the Kostelnička's mother-in-law. More serious is the extent to which this and other cuts reduce the characterisation of the Kostelnička. We are not told that she makes her living by peddling victuals or that her reason for coming to the mill in the first Act is to fetch butter and cheese. Jenůfa's predicament is very much the result of her residing as a house-keeper at the solitary mill, whose only other inhabitants are her senile grandmother, Števa and Laca. In the libretto it is left unexplained that the strictly respectable Kostelnička only allowed this because she trusted them as relatives. Owing to the omission of her reminiscences of her unhappy marriage and of her comparison of Števa to her unworthy husband, the Kostelnička of the libretto is much less complex and sympathetic than the Kostelnička of the drama. In the drama, but not in the libretto, there is a scene in which she is visited by a poor sick widow seeking advice, which shows the Kostelnička as both wise and compassionate. On the whole, the character of the Kostelnička, according to the libretto, can be summed up by the verdict of all the other characters — she is a hard woman. But such was obviously the intention of the composer of whose opera Jenůfa is the heroine. The scene of the Kostelnička with Laca, before she kills the baby, is also a significant departure from the drama. In the drama, after she lies to Laca that the child is dead she goes on to invent details. She tells him that she placed the baby in a little coffin, sprinkled him with holy water and buried him in the cemetery at night. As an afterthought she adds that she christened him herself. In the libretto she simply states several times that the child is dead. This is much more effective even if there is a loss in realistic detail, and Preissová adopted Janáček's cuts in her later version.

After the character of the Kostelnička, Janáček's most radical modification was the character of the village mayor, whom he changed from a despicable boor into a respectable man. In the play it is due to his influence that Števa is declared by the authorities to have attained his majority so that he can take possession of the mill while still under age. In the scene with the recruits the mayor is almost as drunk as Števa, and boasts that he has prevented Števa's being taken into the army and that he has given the recruits a small barrel of his best wine. He is also a hen-pecked husband. His wife scolds him for his roving eye and for associating with spendthrifts, and drags him home after a violent quarrel. All this, which contributes to the social criticism of Preissova's drama, was cut in the libretto.

Finally, Preissová in the concluding monologue addressed to Laca made Jenůfa qualify her high-flown declaration 'only love, greater love which pleases God, has finally led me to you' with the more realistic observation that when she is summoned before the court she will not feel wretched because Laca will be at her side as her husband. But Janáček cut this remark and ended the libretto with an apotheosis of love.

Thus a complex drama composed of interwoven themes — the fate of the characters in a specific society at a specific time, ethical ideas, social criticism — became a drama of passion in accordance with Janáček's belief that love is basically tragic. It was his music that gave it universal and timeless meaning.

The final moment of the 1947 Prague production of 'Katya Kabanova'

The Challenge from Within: Janáček's Musico-dramatic Mastery

Arnold Whittall

The ending of *Katya Kabanova* provides the kind of music which lodges firmly in the mind as archetypal Janáček, the economy of materials and intensity of expression characteristic of his mastery at its most individual. In one respect it is a model of technical orthodoxy: elements from one of the opera's principal thematic ideas are condensed into a conclusive development and resolve into a cadence that combines harmonic completion with thematic clarification. Yet this impression of docile orthodoxy is countered by the extreme concentration with which the composer presents the chain of events: the last (and first) four notes of Kabanicha's final, bitter statement [see *y* in 8b below] are seized on by the orchestra, transposed, and halved then quartered in value, to produce a frenzied ostinato that persists as a strand of the texture to the very end. What is termed 'development' above is in reality more a process of depriving a musical idea of its 'thematic' relevance in order to distil its pure, naked emotion: it becomes a texture which, in hands less sure than Janáček's, could easily seem overblown, hysterical, a simple-minded yielding to the extreme emotions of the moment rather than a suitably weighty conclusion to a powerful and tragic drama. Janáček's ability to transcend mere melodrama so decisively is impressive enough; but that music composed in 1921 should display such an approachable yet original style is, for many listeners in the theatre, more remarkable still.

*   *   *

Janáček's long life spanned a period of momentous change in music: he was born in 1854, the year after Verdi completed *La traviata*, and the year Wagner completed *Das Rheingold*; he died in 1928, three years after the première of *Wozzeck* and one year after Stravinsky completed *Oedipus Rex*. And while it is not difficult to argue that Janáček has more in common with Verdian Romanticism or Bergian Expressionism than with Wagnerian music drama or Stravinskian neo-Classicism, such sweeping comparisons tend to increase our awareness of his great originality. That is not to say that there is never the occasional hint of other, perhaps more familiar, composers; Janáček did, after all, emerge from a Czech tradition dominated by Smetana and Dvořák; while now and again — even as late as *Katya Kabanova* — a richly harmonized cadence or a pentatonic melodic phrase may call Puccini to mind. Janáček certainly shares with the Italian master the ability to achieve a Realism that has little to do with either bombast or vulgarity. Even so, Janáček can scarcely be deemed a Moravian Puccini. He was less cosmopolitan, decadent or sentimental than the composer of *Tosca* and *Madama Butterfly*; and although he was a Realist in shunning the remote or mythological subject-matter associated pre-eminently with German music drama (at least after his first opera *Šarka*) he did not seek to exclude all fantasy or symbolism, as both *The Adventures of Mr Brouček* and *The Cunning Little Vixen* reveal. Above all, Janáček's Realism at its greatest (as both *Jenufa* and *Katya Kabanova* testify) is permeated with a quality best described as visionary: both Jenůfa and Katya have intense inner experiences — fulfilling and destructive respectively —

21

that go far beyond the everyday. And this Realism can accommodate equally effectively the Expressionist outbursts of the Kostelnicka in *Jenůfa* or the folk-style songs of Kudryash and Varvara in *Katya*. The miracle of Janáček lies in the way such diverse elements are brought into coherent co-existence to serve the essence of the drama, through the use of a musical idiom of remarkable flexibility and imagination. Because of his preferred style and subject-matter it may make better sense to term Janáček an opera composer rather than a 'music dramatist'. Yet his music easily transcends the restrictions implied by such a distinction; in particular, it continues the 19th-century practice of extending basic harmonic relations, not in order to force them to breaking point (Janáček was no atonalist) but to enhance their most fundamental properties, expressed most palpably for Janáček — as for Verdi, Wagner, Mussorgsky, Bizet and Puccini, among others — in the distinction, and indissoluble connection, between consonance and dissonance. The heroines of these two operas have more of Puccinian vulnerability than Straussian dominance about them, but the composer himself is a compassionate sceptic, an explorer at the edge of the old world of tonal forms and techniques whose language was the perfect vehicle for these parables of an individual's search for freedom and self-knowledge.

To succeed, operatic music must characterise — people, places, situations — and it must also be organised, providing forms and frameworks to enable the process of characterisation, as it projects the drama, to convey those qualities which enable audiences to recognise and respond to a work of art, rather than an unadulterated 'slice of life'. Janáček's ability to provide vivid musical portraits of vulnerability and viciousness, passion and fecklessness, tenderness and heartiness, is boundless, and needs no translation into words. Yet like all great dramatists he makes the mechanics of organising and manipulating those portraits to produce coherent, large-scale forms as unobtrusive as possible; and he is also a master of evocative, at times unusual, orchestration, his use of the viola d'amore in *Katya* being the best-known example of such originality. The sustained pictorial intensity of the storm music in Act Three of *Katya* is probably the most spectacular instance in these two operas of an art which never forces itself on the listener's attention (the means never distracting from the ends) yet which for that very reason is of absorbing facination to anyone who, enslaved by the sheer brilliance of the result, wishes to discover exactly how such magic has been achieved. Janáček's particular skill was to use the simplest elements of melody and harmony, as well as textures which can, out of context, seem dangerously unsophisticated, to reflect the disturbances of minds constrained by convention. Thus musical elements which can, and are, especially well designed to create a comforting sense of security tend, in Janáček's hands, to subvert security, even if, as is ultimately the case in *Jenůfa*, the outcome is strongly positive. Janáček's 'moral', then, is that what is right is to transform convention from within — not simply to reject it, or seek to destroy it from outside. Katya's tragedy is that she forces confrontation, and finds self-destruction rather than self-realisation. In *Jenůfa* it is the Kostelnička whose guilt-ridden destructiveness enables Jenůfa herself to achieve self-knowledge and the prospect of a new, more rewarding life. It may be flirting with absurdity to reduce these subjects to such rudimentary psychological slogans, but it does no harm to use the point to reinforce the argument that the composer's own attitude to musical tradition — and the long apprenticeship which, in the end, enabled him to transform it — was likely to lead him to such dramatic themes: subjects and music are made for each other.

Patricia Johnson as Kostelnička in the 1977 production of 'Jenůfa' at Covent Garden; producer, Ande Anderson; designer, Jan Brazda (photo: Christina Burton)

It is often implied, and even occasionally stated, that any discussion of Janáček's operas which is primarily concerned with music rather than text is by definition irrelevant. With this composer, it is claimed, the rhythm, colour and character of the Czech libretto is everything, and the music is merely the means to ensure that textual rhythm, colour and character make the maximum impact. Of course, the argument about whether music or words come first in opera is as old as opera itself, and is normally resolved by pointing out that even in cases where a composer has a complete libretto to hand before a single musical idea occurs to him, the process of musical setting most frequently has the effect of (literally) setting the text in a context greater than itself. In Janáček's case, certainly, it seems undeniable that however much importance he attached to textual features, the function of that text was to stimulate his musical invention. The music may indeed translate fundamental aspects of the text into its own terms, but it then uses that translation to build musical forms and to achieve musical effects which do much more than provide vocal lines with unobtrusive accompaniments. The text is by no means submerged in music, but it is enhanced by it, and in a very striking way. Janáček makes much use of declamatory 'arioso': lines of text are set to expressive melodic shapes placed against a continuous orchestral accompaniment, rather than combining to make up conventionally balanced phrases after the model of the traditional aria. This is a basic technique that Janáček shares with most other post-Classical opera composers, and it is in determining the contour and rhythmic profile of these phrases, irrespective of their accompaniment, that the character of the text is most influential. It is in the more folk-like episodes and set-pieces that the vocal phrases are most regular, but here, of course, that folk-like quality does much to keep such sections at a considerable remove from what might normally be termed an 'aria'.

*   *   *

It took Janáček a long time to emerge from the shadows of predecessors and traditions, and even the first act of *Jenůfa*, his third opera, composed between early 1895 (Janáček's 41st year) and 1897, may seem relatively immature — not in the sense of being derivative, but displaying a certain lack of focus of musical ideas and substance, compared with the later acts and the later operas. The whole work was completed in January 1903, and even after the revisions made in 1908 — apparently to reduce any sense of the survival of traditional 'numbers' — the impression remains of a composer possibly still undecided about how 'radical' his style should be, in shunning easily graspable melodic motifs and regular phrase structures. Where Janáček seems least at ease, and where the style of *Jenůfa*, Act One, is most redolent of earlier conventions, is in the ensemble at the end of Scene Five. And the composer's decision to make a substantial cut in the Kostelnička's entrance 'aria' earlier in the same scene, while it removes some relatively ordinary music and ensures that the emphasis shifts less decisively away from Jenůfa herself, leaves the vital character of the Kostelnička too ill-defined. A particularly effective device in this act is the transformation of the artless little tune associated with Jenůfa in Scene One [1a] and used by her at the start of Scene Five into the heartless folk-like chorus (with Steva) later in Scene Five [1b], which graphically emphasises Jenůfa's alienation from collective village jollifications. The final, hectic orchestral version of this tune, accompanying a dance, leads up to the crucial moment of the Kostelnička's entrance, in a structural conjunction of juxtaposition and continuity as pointed as any in the later Janáček [1c].

There is perhaps even a case for suggesting that the later, fully focussed Janáček is in some respects a more 'conservative' figure than the Janáček of 1895-7. And if the composer himself was dissatisfied with aspects of Act One of *Jenůfa*, it may have had something to do with a feeling that the music was being less than ideally faithful to the text (if not to the drama). As John Tyrrell has pointed out, *Jenůfa* and its predecessor, *The Beginning of a Romance*, are both set 'in the same world of Moravian Slovakia and both offer the same potential for the use of its folk music'. But whereas *The Beginning of a Romance* is 'little more than an operatic manifestation of Janáček's then current preoccupation with popularising Moravian folk tunes by kitting them out with opulent orchestrations and building them up into larger forms', *Jenůfa* sees the beginning of that process of holding authentic folk tunes at a distance in order to allow their musical essences to operate at an altogether deeper and more satisfying level. If Janáček was to compose with the elements of folk style rather than merely to arrange folk music, then a considerable adjustment was needed, and in Act One of *Jenůfa* that process of adjustment was still incomplete. Both *Jenůfa* and *Katya* contain tunes whose poignant artlessness seems to guarantee an authentic folk origin [1b, 10b, 13], and the Bridal Chorus from *Jenůfa* Act Three [see 5a below] has actually been included in folk music anthologies. The fact that it is more probably an imitation than the genuine article does not make it any the less folk-like, of course, but Janáček may well have felt that he would be able to move more

24

naturally into and out of such an episode — away from and back to his own musical style — with greater conviction and inevitability if he did not literally quote an existing folk tune. No doubt he could have achieved the same result with such an existing tune, but like any great composer he was fascinated by essences, and the greater creative challenge involved in what is, in the best sense, pastiche, and its integration into a coherent, large-scale musical structure.

Whatever one's criticisms of *Jenůfa* Act One, it cannot be denied that it already displays a forceful economy of gesture that provides a powerful impetus for particular episodes: the three-quaver figure that launches Laca's first solo and the inversion of it that features prominently in Jenůfa's own subsequent music (both deriving from 1a) are both elementary in the extreme [*x* in 2a and b]: but Janáček's vigorous exploitation of them (and the polarity between their reiterations and the large-scale features of melody and harmony) is of the kind that no other composer of this time would have dared to risk — save possibly Puccini — and gives them ample musico-dramatic validity. Act Two nevertheless marks a notable gain in musico-dramatic cogency, with the contrast between the Kostelnička and Jenůfa herself brought fully into focus, and the Kostelnička's contradictory blend of tenderness and ferocity, love and bitterness, powerfully conveyed. Here too Janáček's ability to create dramatic accompaniments and contexts out of evolving combinations of simple ostinati is already fully evident as, for example, in the build-up to the climax of Scene Five as the Kostelnička decides to do away with Jenůfa's child. But the orchestra can also take the lead, as in the extraordinarily moving, restrained passage in Scene Seven where Jenůfa laments the child's death, and the music [3] creates an atmosphere of grief as memorable as anything in Janáček's entire output. A final example from Act Two of the dramatic force of music in which the prime function of the orchestra is to support vocal characterisation and to engineer transitions in the most economical and effective fashion possible is provided by the end of Scene Six and the beginning of Scene Seven. At the end of her long monologue Jenůfa prays to the Virgin to protect her son: a passage with ample potential for the most mawkish sentimentality which Janáček avoids by sheer restraint. The accompanying harmony changes only very slowly, articulated by ostinati which move at different speeds and by a melodic line which selects all its elements from the accompaniment but gives them broader melodic perspective. The point at which the harmony returns to its starting point (four bars after Fig. 77 in the score) [4a] is the point at which mood and material begin to change, and by the simple device of freezing the accompaniment into a single chord and treating it as a tremolo while a new motif in the orchestra springs directly from a vocal phrase (the last bar before Fig. 78) [4b] Janáček rapidly effects an extreme change of mood, from serenity to fear and menace, with harrowing and totally convincing realism.

As a whole *Jenůfa* displays a style and form ideally matched to the representation of the intimate, claustrophobic interactions of village life; there is a wealth of short ensembles and solo sections which creates the need for the music to sustain continuity through the use of economical transitions. One such passage from Act Two has just been discussed, but it is Act Three, with its great climax, which offers the richest instances of Janáček's stylistic individuality, as well as his mastery of musical form. The Bridal Chorus represents the composer's mature musical language at its most memorably direct. One-bar units in the accompaniment support the regular four-bar phrases of the song [see 5a], whose main motif echoes *y* in [2b]; but added

25

chromatic notes in the melody and harmony prevent the music from settling into an utterly straightforward diatonic mould, and an added bar at the end of each stanza breaks the regular phrase-structure with equal pointedness. So far, so simple: yet this short episode is far from isolated from its musical surroundings in Act Three — Janáček's mastery of that most 19th-century (and most Wagnerian) of operatic techniques, the art of transition, is even more powerfully evident after the Bridal Chorus than before it. The composer's technique (and its processes, it must be stressed, are eminently audible: no analytical, intellectual manipulation of the actual music is required to identify it) is to reduce the accompaniment to the barest outline of the folk-like motif while unobtrusively shifting its harmonic centre from D to F sharp to prepare the next principal tonal area (G flat, Fig. 37). At the same time, the melodic line loses its folk-like regularity, as Laca and Jenůfa return to the centre of the action. During the brief blessing from Jenůfa's grandmother the Bridal Chorus motif, now compressed within a single crotchet beat, continues to be heard, but it finally dissolves into the register of the horn call that provides the mayor with the notes for his straightfoward but (musically) crucial transitional phrase [5b].

Details like these are so important to a full appreciation of Janáček's art simply because they give conclusive evidence of his ability to provide that feature on which all through-composed opera depends for its coherence, and therefore its success: the interaction of large- and small-scale factors; the large-scale tonal areas and formal units in which particular thematic ideas predominate, and the brief, often unobtrusive moments of change between these areas which ensure the evolution of the drama as something inevitable, and, therefore, as dramatically convincing rather than merely arbitrary and artificial. Nowhere is Janáček's confident handling of a large-scale musical background as framework for momentous dramatic developments more evident, even to the casual listener, than in the last two scenes of *Jenůfa*. Here Jenůfa herself is the central figure, and we move quickly from her understated, gentle words of forgiveness to the Kostelnička to her outburst of exultation when she realises that Laca's love for her has been strengthened and not destroyed by the terrible events just revealed. The single but extreme emotional progression is symbolised musically by a tonal progression from a starting point (E major, Fig. 55 — a chord rather than a key, it should be noted) to a finishing point of considerable harmonic remoteness — E flat major (established as a key at Fig. 66). Janáček treats this scheme not as a mechanism which merely needs to be set in motion to achieve the desired result — as would happen, for example, if a segment of the cycle of fifths were invoked, and the music moved through E, A, D, G, C, F and B flat on to E flat. What the drama requires is a *double* progression: first, to resolve the relationship between Jenůfa and the Kostelnička, in which Jenůfa herself progresses from inner serenity to a rhetorical (but utterly convincing) affirmation of the power of redemption — an affirmation echoed by the Kostelnička herself; second, to answer Jenůfa's own doubts about the attitude and the feelings of Laca — a progression from uncertainty to supreme joy. Janáček's solution to the need to balance inevitability with unpredictability is masterly; for the last exchanges with the Kostelnička he initiates what is, in essence, a cycle-of-fifths progression: E major, A major (Fig. 56) moving directly to D major four bars later, but then, after only three bars, skipping a stage and moving straight to C major for Jenůfa's exclamation — 'The Saviour will look down on her!' [6]. This 'skip' is the perfect musical metaphor for Jenůfa's impulsive gesture of forgiveness, but having made the

26

leap Janáček redresses the balance, centering the remainder of the scene on the mixture of C major and C minor, with the additional subtlety of a move (at Fig. 58) which could prepare a return to the E major chord from which the scene started out, but is in fact used instead to prepare the second and still more powerfully emphasised C major triad. Here, as at the end of the final scene itself, Janáček allows the orchestra to complete what is beyond words — in this case the Kostelnička's response to Jenůfa's injunction 'God give you comfort', in an overwhelming orchestral crescendo which not only flirts with musical hyperbole but runs the further risk of leaving all that follows as anti-climactic. That neither of these things happens is further proof of Janáček's genius — his instinct for how to make the boldest musical gestures seem dramatically the truest.

Elisabeth Söderström as Jenůfa in the Royal Opera of Stockholm production that toured to the Edinburgh Festival in 1974 (photo: Enar Merkel Rydberg)

The musical metaphor for the final scene's progress from doubt to certainty, as a direct outcome of the events of Scene Eleven, is also sublimely simple. Janáček retains the bass note, C, which has dominated Scene Eleven, but places questing, unstable harmony above it, never the pure major triad. As Laca's wish to stay with Jenůfa becomes clear the harmony gains in radiance (and in E flat major diatonicism) without resolving on to the tonic chord of E flat itself, and it is only at the start of Jenůfa's own final eight-bar phrase, based primarily on the notes of the B flat major triad, that the bass falls the step from C to B flat in preparation for the final resolution. Jenůfa's final outpouring of joy is the more effective for its brevity, and for the way it leaves the ultimate fulfilment of resolution to the orchestra [7]. This is indeed a joy beyond words, and the sense of reaching beyond the events of the opera itself is the greater in view of the fact that the key of E flat major has not appeared in the work before these final bars. The power of this resolution is overwhelming in Janáček's original version, and it is difficult not to feel that the more familiar version by Karel Kovařovic, with the melody in canon, is simply too much of a good thing. For it is above all the majesty and daring simplicity of

27

these final scenes, where Janáček employs the most forceful rhetoric without descending into bombast or melodrama, which make *Jenůfa* the great theatrical experience it is.

* * *

The common ground between *Jenůfa* and *Katya Kabanova* is easy to perceive. Both are tragedies; *Jenůfa* happens to have a 'happy ending', but a happy ending placing the tragedy of the Kostelnicka in far more powerful relief than, for example, a melodramatic conclusion in which Jenůfa herself died of grief would be likely to do. Both operas hinge on the contrast between the two principal female characters, and it is undeniable that this confrontation is more effectively realised in *Katya* than in *Jenůfa*. As has often been argued the Kostelnička is really the principal character of the earlier opera, rather than Jenůfa herself. But even when some of Janáček's later cuts in her part are restored (as in the Mackerras recording for Decca) there is still at times a feeling that the composer is relying too much on mere vocal gesture, rather than fully shaped musical ideas, to portray her. The confrontation between Katya and Kabanicha in the later opera is more successful in purely musical terms, not least because there is never any doubt that it is Katya herself who is the true protagonist. Her music is quite different from that of any other character in the work; as John Tyrrell sees it, in his essay accompanying the Decca recording, she 'is the only character with flexible, distinctive music which changes and grows with her during the opera'. It could indeed be a weakness that every other character, even Kabanicha, remains in Tyrrell's words 'a two-dimensional caricature': but in a work of such economy the effect is far from unsatisfactory, since in a sense we see the whole sequence of events through Katya's eyes, and the other characters are as they seem to her rather than as they might be portrayed by a more objective, detached observer.

To compare the ways in which *Katya* uses the same types of musical material and process as *Jenůfa* is to appreciate how much of genuine potential was already so well realised in the earlier work. Not surprisingly, nevertheless, Janáček shows even more decisive mastery in *Katya* in his handling of such all-important devices as the transition between folk-like material and other features, as well as in the formal balancing of juxtaposition and integration. At the very beginning, in the orchestral introduction to Act One, the timpani motif [8a] which so clearly speaks of menace, fate and despair, provides common ground between the first section's plaintive material, representing Katya's vulnerability, her tragic openness to emotion, and the lively pentatonic theme of the second section [8b], whose associations are in part with travel (Tichon's departure at the end of Act One) but more fundamentally, it seems, with the whole notion of escape, of flight into freedom. As if in awareness of the degree to which such a linking motif might create a glib, superficial kind of organicism, Janáček plays on the listener's expectations here in a very striking way. At the end of the first section the turning woodwind figure suddenly breaks loose to begin what could be a brief transition to the second section, using Janáček's favourite device of transforming simple melody into hectic ostinato. But instead of running this transition straight into the second section, as could perfectly well happen, the composer opts instead for a decisive cadential conclusion to Section 1 — a loud statement of the 'Fate' motif [8a] at the original tempo. Section 2 then begins at a much faster tempo and with a very different texture. Even so, the basic tonality remains the same as before (B flat minor) and the new motif [8b] grows very directly out of the 'Fate' theme itself [see x in 8a and b]. In this way juxtaposition and integration, transposition and contrast, are all brought together to create a highly dramatic effect. Katya's capacity for tenderness and her desire for escape are shown to be both related and in conflict. From this tension the tragedy will spring.

To do justice even to any one aspect of a score as rich as *Katya* in a brief space is impossible, but a study of the way in which Act Two deals on a larger scale with the kind of dramatic structural principles referred to in connection with the opening of Act One should at least serve to emphasise and clarify some of the basic elements of Janáček's originality, the sources of his fascination. In Act Two, just over half an hour of music, we have the enactment of Katya's adultery, presented in a way that cruelly highlights the conflict between ecstasy and guilt, honour and narrow-mindedness. Katya and Boris are nothing if not creatures of impulse, drawn together by their ability to yield to their deepest feelings, though very different in their reactions to the consequences of such yielding. It is therefore appropriate that the soaring phrases of their love scene should show Janáček at his most 'Romantic', the music asking fewer questions of itself than usual, yet still shunning any sense of artifically whipped-up rhetoric. It is in fact the second couple, Varvara and Kudryash, who are in a way more crucial to the development and tone of the drama here, embodying a vital ambiguity which the text suggests but the music renders powerfully explicit. On the one hand, they seem the very model of the cheerful rural courting couple, not in the least bothered by the conventions that hem them in, and appropriately expressing themselves in artless, folk-like songs. At the same time they function as tempters and even, to a degree, taunters of the more self-conscious, guilty lovers. In the first scene it is Varvara who encourages Katya to take the key which will enable her to get back into the house after her meeting with Boris, and although Kudryash later warns Boris of the likely consequences he joins Varvara in encouraging Katya and Boris to 'take a walk together'. Varvara and Kudryash then summon the lovers back with a beautiful but at the same time bitterly ironic song, while Varvara has the last line of the act — 'Can't you say goodbye to each other?' — addressed to Katya and Boris — a line that seems perfectly poised between the concerned and the callous. In this way, although Katya's main antagonist, her mother-in-law Kabanicha, is not directly involved in these events, it is as if Varvara (a Kabanov foster child — an actual daughter in the original play) and her boy-friend are acting, wittingly or not, as surrogates for those who will Katya's destruction. Musically this situation gives the composer the maximum opportunity to play off very strongly contrasted types of material against one another while never losing sight of the fact that they are necessarily connected: the essence of the tragedy is that the one attitude (or type of idea) implies and requires the other, and so the music must reach behind simple contrasts for connections and interactions.

At an early stage of Scene One (Fig 3) there is a clear contrast between the orchestral statement (following Kabanicha's departure) of a theme redolent of Katya's anguish and frustration and the bouncy repetitions of Varvara's music [9a]. But it is the 'anguish' idea which Varvara's own first vocal phrase echoes [9b], and as this part of the scene proceeds, Janáček develops the two types of material side by side in the orchestra, to reinforce the sense of interdependence that exists between Katya's misery and Varvara's lightheartedness. A comparable drawing of interdependence out of juxtaposition comes at the beginning of Scene Two. The orchestral interlude (itself juxtaposing two very different types of material) is dominated by questing, chromatic surges [10a] that provide a generative model for Kudryash's folk-like song [10b — compare 1b above!], whose forceful rather than lyrical phrases, for all their rhythmic regularity, seem to have a latent menace in their modal instability. Thus it comes as no surprise when this material provides a clear and convincing link back to the questing chromatics as Boris appears.

Juxtaposition is at its clearest in the contrast between the song Varvara and Kudryash share at Varvara's entrance (Fig. 10) and the questing music which frames it, leading to the entrance of Katya herself. And the rest of the act, dominated by the love duet and its aftermath, is an oustanding demonstration of how Janáček can integrate contrasts without depriving the contrasted elements of their necessary independence. The love duet itself is dominated by a single, arching motif of supreme eloquence [11a], which appears in a great variety of instantly identifiable versions, and it easily yields the very different shape which accompanies the comments of Varvara and Kudryash (see in particular the passage before and after Fig. 24) [11b]. This stage of the drama reaches its climax when music for the two pairs is superimposed, and their spatial separation is enhanced by the combination of two very different (though harmonically completely compatible) melodic phrases (five bars after Fig. 26). And now the scene is set for the final stage of Act Two. After Fig. 29 — one phrase for Boris apart — it is left to the orchestra to express the emotions of the lovers, and the last two bars of the orchestral music give Kudryash the cue for his beautiful, and beautifully ironic, song calling the lovers home [12]. The irony is compounded by the melodic link to the 'escape' motif, discussed earlier [x in 8b and 12]. In itself, the song could hardly be more straightforward — an eight-bar phrase stated by Kudryash [13], taken up by Varvara and then repeated by Kudryash. Needless to say, however, the one thing Janáček does not do is place this three-stanza song in isolation, in quotation marks, with clear breaks before and after. The way it grows out of the orchestral love music has already been described, and at the end the moment of clear cadence is also the moment where the harmony turns sour. A minor chord supports Varvara's last question, and then the music heaves itself from reflective D flat minor to passionate E major, returning to, and further developing, the turning figure associated with the love of Katya and Boris (bars 1 and 2 of [12]).

Perhaps the most 'realistic' aspect of Act Two is that, despite the intensity of their feelings, Boris and Katya are never idealised, just as Varvara and Kudryash are never merely a lovable comic pair — they are no Papagena and Papageno. The twists and turns of Janáček's musical fabric remain unerringly under control as the drama evolves; if the essence of that drama is in confrontation, the essence of the structure of the work of art is in the coherent balance between elements which could simply diverge and co-exist without dramatic interaction. In this sense Janáček's greatness as an opera composer is that of all other great opera composers: but the remarkable originality of his style, and the striking contrasts evident between, for example, the artless Bridal Chorus and the consequent high tension and final exaltation in *Jenůfa*, or between Kudryash's song and the love music in Act Two of *Katya*, indicate why, in becoming aware of that greatness, we are never likely to confuse Janáček with any other operatic master.

Thematic Guide

[1a]

Allegro

Oboe

ppp

[1b]

STEVA

Con moto

f

Da – le – ko   ši – ro – ko   do těch No – vých Zám – ků;
Far a – way   there in   the town of No – vých Zám – ků

[1c]

Vivace

tr

ff   *sf*   *sf*

sf

[2a]

Allegro

LACA

Vy,   sta-řen-ko,
Yes,   Gran-ny dear,

f   *pp*

[2b]

JENUFA

Moderato

Sta – řen – ko,   ne-hně-vej-te se,
Grand-ma, dear,   do not be up-set!

p

31

JENUFA
Moderato

toż   u___mřel můj ch'ap-čok ra-dost-ný___
he   died_then, my dar-ling ba-by boy,___

[4a]

JÉNUFA
Moderato

o pře-slad-ká Pan-no Ma-ri-a!   A Ste-vuš-ka mi ochraňuj
O most sweet Vir-gin Ma-ry !   And Ste-vuš-ka protect for me

[4b]

JENUFA

Con moto

mat-ko mi-lo-sr-den-stŭl!
O most mer-ci-ful mo-ther!

[5a]
CHORUS
Allegro

Ej mam-ko, mam — ko, ma – měn - ko mo – ja!
Hey, mo-ther, mo — ther, lit - tle mo-ther mine!

[5b]

leading to   and to

MAYOR

vy to a – si do-ká že - te   jak ve-leb-ní-ček!
would know the way to do it as   the priest would do it!

[6]
JENUFA
Largo

A - ji na ni   Spa-si - tel po-hléd-ne!
The Sa-viour   will look down on her!

[7] (orchestral accompaniment in outline only)
JENUFA
Moderato

Pán _____ bůh ____ sní spo-ko-jen!
God _____ give ____ you com-fort

cresc. sempre

33

[8a]

Moderato

[8b]

Allegro

[9a]

leading to

Allegretto

[9b]

VARVARA

Allegretto

Půj‐du též se pro‐jit
It's so warm in‐doors

[10a]

Moderato

[10b]

KUDRYASH

Allegro

Po za‐hrád‐ce dě‐vu‐cha‐již rá‐no se pro‐chá‐ze‐la,
One day ear‐ly by the ri‐ver wal‐ked a love‐ly mai‐den

34

[11a]

[11b] *(outline only)*

un poco piu mosso

[12]

Lento

Allegretto

KUDRYASH

Všec-ko do - mů, do - mů
Home-ward all good peo-ple,

Všec-ko do - mů, do - mů
home-ward all good peo-ple

[13]

KUDRYASH

Allegretto

Chod' si div - ka do ča - su do ve - čer - ní - ho ča - su
It is night and far from home mai-dens should no lon - ger roam.

Ei, le - li, le - li, le - li, do ve - čer - ní - ho ča - su.
Ei, le - li, le - li, le - li, mai-dens should no lon - ger roam.

35

Janáček and Czech Realism

Jan Smaczny

If the sources of Janáček's highly individual musical style are difficult to fathom, the operatic tradition which stands in the background to his earlier operas is rather easier to discern. While the Prague National Theatre was still the nation's 'artistic hearth and home'[1] in the 1890s, the repertoire of Czech operas which had been built up since the opening of the Provisional Theatre in the 1860s had changed considerably in nature. The historical-mythological and naive comic operas of the Theatre's early years were gradually being supplanted by the new realism which was sweeping Europe in the 1890s. Janáček had dabbled with both the traditional styles of Czech opera in his first two attempts at the genre: Šarka — based on the amazonic warriors of Czech legend — and the rural comedy The Beginning of a Romance. By the 1890s there was a perceptible shift of emphasis towards veristic subject matter. Even old hands, such as Karel Bendl and Josef Rozkošný who had done much to establish the familiar trends in Czech opera, were turning to the new style from France and Italy. Dvořák and Fibich were among the few who stood apart from their contemporaries. With their reputations secure they were content to pursue their own inclinations, none of which led to realistic subjects.

Finding categories for the large variety of operas composed and staged in Bohemia and Moravia in the last twelve or so years of the 19th century is not the easiest of tasks. Of the older types of opera cultivated by Czech composers, the naive rural comedy still maintained a footing, with Dvořák's The Devil and Kate standing as the most successful representative of a tradition which stretches back to The Bartered Bride. The other pillar of Czech operatic art, the historical-mythological strain nurtured by Smetana, Šebor and Bendl in the 1860s and 1870s, continued well into the 20th century with Otakar Ostrčil's The Passing of Vlasta, although Fibich's Šarka is probably the most distinguished representative of the genre from the 1890s. But the day of the impassioned and dignified national statement was fast disappearing (in some ways Janáček's Adventures of Mr Brouček almost seems an unconscious parody of the type) and composers were increasingly turning to more contemporary themes. Of the nearly fifty operas produced by Czech composers at the turn of the century the folkloric element was represented by six operas, including Dvořák's Rusalka. The historical-mythological types comprised a similar number and Realist operas amounted to sixteen. These ranged from the countrified drama of Bendl's Mother Dear and Foerster's Eva to Jindřich Káan's setting of Zola's Germinal. Germinal was something of an exception, however, because the main feature of the new Czech Realism was its rural setting; the idealised country-folk of Smetana's comedies and 'simple-national' (prostonárodní) operas belonged to the years when Czech national opera was establishing its credentials. The serpent had crept into the garden with the plays of Gabriela Preissová, and was firmly domiciled by the mid-1890s. Even Dvořák's comedy The Devil and Kate has an earthy realism in the portrayal of character, and it remained the only Czech comic opera to

1 Karel Hoffmeister, Antonin Dvořák, trans. R. Newmarch, London 1928.

avoid any love interest in the plot. Another feature of the repertoire in the 1890s was the increase in the number of operas based on foreign literature. These included four settings of Shakespeare, one of Tasso (Dvořák's *Armida*) and one of Byron (Fibich's *Hedy*). Horizons were broadening, and a work like Roman Nejedly's *Andulka* in the 'simple-national' tradition of Smetana's *Hubička* was something of a stranger in the ranks of the more febrile heroines of Czech verismo.

One of the most successful of the new Realist operas was Josef Foerster's *Eva*. Like *Jenůfa* it was based on a play by Gabriela Preissová. Foerster had seen the première of *Her Foster-Daughter* on November 9, 1890, but opted to set a play which had been premièred the previous year on November 7, 1889, *The Farmer's Woman*. Preissová was quite happy for Foerster to turn her play into an opera and, as a matter of course, suggested a poet, Jaroslav Kvapil (the librettist of Dvořák's *Rusalka*), as a possible collaborator. After three years of inaction Foerster took the law into his own hands and produced his own versified text. The assumption was that verse was the only way of rendering a text singable. While Foerster was not without talent as a versifier, the short, rather trite lines he adopted for *Eva* seriously hamper the dramatic flow and threaten to reduce even climactic scenes to near hilarity. This, and the inadequate motivation for the characters, mean that *Eva* is unlikely to gain a foothold in the modern repertoire abroad, while in Czechoslovakia it still remains a rarity, despite its initial popularity. The strength of Janáček's second Preissová opera, *Jenůfa*, (*The Beginning of a Romance* was based on a short story from a group entitled *Pictures from Moravian-Slovakia* which Preissová had published between 1886 and 1889) lies in the stronger motivation and, above all, in the prose text. Where the conventionalised verse forms of *Eva* had inhibited the drama, compelling Foerster to supply balanced melodic phrases, the free flow of the text in *Jenůfa* enabled Janáček to maintain the force of a dramatic situation throughout. The composer subjected the play to very little modification and left the abruptness of much of the dialogue in its original form. Adopting, rather than adapting, the rough edges and repetitions of the play did much to enhance the realistic portrayal of character and situation. Although Bruneau and Mussorgsky had followed a similar path, Janáček, as the programme of the first performance of *Jenůfa* pointed out, took the step on his own initiative.

Far from providing a tragic alternative to *The Bartered Bride*, Preissová's play was a genuinely new departure for the Czech stage as the opposition from conservative quarters to both *The Farmer's Woman* and *Her Foster-Daughter* evinced. The idea of rural goings-on providing a suitable background to national opera was almost as old as the Czech national revival itself. Small country towns or villages were the invariable settings for Czech comic operas. There was a tradition of plays based on 'pictures of country life', sometimes with 'living tableaux', going back to the 1860s. The difference between these rather anodyne productions and *Her Foster-Daughter* was the word 'drama'. The subtitle of Preissová's play was 'drama from Moravian country life', and the seriousness of its subject matter was its principal novel feature. The playwright encountered much hostile criticism from those who clung to an ideal notion of rustic life. But having spent nearly ten years among the people with whom she was dealing in her plays, the veracity of her treatment of the darker corners of life in the country was based on genuine experience. *Her Foster-Daughter* was inspired by actual events recorded in the local press; later she was to lecture on the peasant background to her plays.

37

The Scottish Opera production of Jenůfa by David Pountney, designed by Maria Björnson, with Gregory Dempsey as Števa (photo: Eric Thorburn)

Janáček observed the new, hard edge perceptible in the play by abandoning, to a large extent, the folk elements he had cultivated in *The Beginning of a Romance*. Having made extensive use of both the music and the words of folk songs in this early opera, he may well have worked the authentic folk style out of his system. In *Jenůfa* the only parts which relate directly to folk style come in Acts One and Three. The recruiting chorus and dance, and the bridal chorus of Act Three, are clearly founded on Janáček's experience of folk song. While both can be seen as vestiges of the Czech obsession with ballet in opera, neither is entirely ornamental. The recruiting chorus is especially vital in setting off the entry of the Kostelnička, and the bridal chorus in Act Three does much to enhance the tension and irony of Jenůfa's wedding. But even these elements are pared away in Act Two, where nothing is allowed to distract from the action's claustrophobic intensity.

Janáček's Czech biographer Jaroslav Vogel, was inclined to dismiss Italian verismo as an important constituent of the background to *Jenůfa*. The resemblance between Turiddu and Števa, Santuzza and Jenůfa is of far less importance than the nature of the subject-matter and its realistic setting. The music of Mascagni and Puccini was well known to Czech opera audiences. Dvořák had complained of the National Theatre's bias towards foreign novelties, although he took a slightly prurient interest in Gustave Charpentier's *Louise*. Janáček also recorded[2] that Dvořák's *Armida* would have been his last work to adopt archaic conventions, although the sketches that remain of *Horimýr* do not suggest a major change of direction. Most of the standard

2 Leoš Janáček, 'Za Antoninem Dvořákem', in *Hudební revue*, Prague, October 1911.

works of the Italian verismo repertoire were quickly taken into the repertoire of the National Theatre in Prague once they had been translated into Czech. *Cavalleria rusticana* was premièred in January 1891, followed by *I Pagliacci* in February 1893. *La Bohème* was given in 1898 and the first unveiling of *Jenůfa* on January 21, 1904 in Brno was followed the next night by a performance of *Tosca*. With so many verismo works in the repertoire of the National Theatre it would be surprising if their influence had not made itself felt in *Jenůfa*. As early as 1897 a hint of verismo colouring had done much to warm up the more passionate episodes in Act Two of Fibich's *Šárka*. In *Jenůfa*, Janáček was as successful in eschewing ornamental or irrelevant lyricism as he was in excluding the inappropriate folk style, but in places a distinctly Italianate melodic element does emerge. The theme which steals in over the pulsating accompaniment in the final scene of Act Three of *Jenůfa* has a distinct affinity, whether conscious or not, with Puccini:

Jenůfa Act Three, scene twelve

Puccini: *La Bohème* Act Four

Janáček scores, however, by using his lyrical fragment as part of a greater climax, rather than as a climax in itself. Elsewhere, his ability to prolong a moment of drama without recourse to melodrama sets him apart from the originators of verismo. For instance, the way he only resolves the long held C, which underpins the first part of the Act Three finale, at the crucial moment in the duet when Jenůfa mentions Laca's name is magnificent in maintaining the tension. Equally effective is the conclusion of Act Two, where the orchestra draws out the horror felt by the Kostelnička.

The realism of Janáček's treatment of *Jenůfa* was, of course, greatly dependent on his word-setting. The alterations which Janáček made to the basic text did little to alter the force of the details of Preissová's original. Janáček's ear for realistic speech and dialogue was unrivalled amongst his Czech contemporaries. The melody generated by the transfer of speech to musical notation was a technique well known to a number of 19th-century composers, although none pursued the theory with anything like the intensity of Janáček, who filled numerous books of manuscript with human and animal sounds. John Tyrrell[3] has questioned the extent and importance of speech-melody in Janáček's operas. While Janáček's heightened experience of the realities of spoken Czech and, in the case of *Jenůfa*, Moravian dialect was important in leading him towards credible declamation, the variety of ways in which he sets the proper names in the opera, notwithstanding changes in the emotional situation, hardly suggests rigidity. Even by the 1890s, with some thirty years of operatic settings of Czech behind them, composers still had difficulties in dealing with their own language. Dvořák, for instance, who unlike Smetana was brought up speaking Czech, had problems as late as his last three operas in reconciling his melodic inspiration with idiomatic declamation. By avoiding a strictly metrical text with its consequent need for balanced lyrical phrases — Dvořák's frequent jibes to Janáček that there was too little melody in his music suggest a fundamental difference in musical make-up — Janáček side-stepped the conventionalised melodic style which makes Foerster's *Eva* such a compromised work.

Janáček's next two operas, *Fate* and *The Adventures of Mr Brouček*, do not stand in the same tradition as *Jenůfa*. Despite the emotional connection with Čelanský's *Kamilla*, *Fate* plots the course of a peculiarly personal catharsis which simply does not fall into any of the familiar categories. *Brouček*, too, is remote from contemporary traditions of Czech opera, although its subject matter was more familiar to theatre audiences from a farce staged in the National Theatre in Prague in November, 1894. At first sight *Katya Kabanova* appears to be a return to the manner of *Jenůfa* with its concentration on two main female characters. The fact that it was based on a Czech translation of a Russian play also draws *Katya* closer to the traditions of Czech opera as they were developing at the turn of the century when novels by Sienkiewicz, Zola and Gogol provided the literary background for a number of works. Yet, as Janáček acknowledged, his heroine was gentle by nature and the tragedy which eventually transforms Jenůfa's world into one of ecstasy, destroys Katya. If the subtlety of Janáček's characterisation were ignored, then *Katya* might be felt to inhabit a similar world to *Eva*, since both heroines commit suicide by throwing themselves into rivers. But where motivation seems to be almost entirely lacking in *Eva* it is one of the triumphs of *Katya*. In the careful delineation of character and feeling for atmosphere, Janáček's later opera can genuinely be described as Realist, although once again it cannot easily be categorised. With *Jenůfa* Janáček provided a personal response to an existing trend in contemporary Czech theatre and opera. At the same time his approach was so challenging, novel and uncompromising that it placed the work outside the tradition to which, superficially, it seemed to belong. If *Katya* seems to be something of a return to the straight and narrow after the explorations of *Fate* and *Mr Brouček*, its singular qualities, like those of *Jenůfa*, place it in a category of its own. The beginning of the journey is familiar enough territory, but the end is an entirely different world.

3 John Tyrrell, 'Janáček and the speech-melody myth', *The Musical Times*, August 1970.

Jenůfa
(Her Foster-Daughter)

Opera in Three Acts
by Leoš Janáček

Text by the composer after 'Scenes from Moravian
Peasant Life' by Gabriela Preissová

English translation by Otakar Kraus and Edward Downes

Jenůfa (*Její Pastorkyňa*) was first performed in Brno on January 21, 1904. It was first performed in the United States in New York at the Metropolitan Opera House (in German) on December 6, 1924. The first performance in Britain was at The Royal Opera House, Covent Garden (in English) on December 10, 1956.

Both *Jenůfa* and *Katya Kabanova* were written in prose and are in verse only where there are actual songs in the action. We have arranged the lines in these texts, however, so as to align the English with the Czech.

Grandmother Buryja		*contralto*
Laca Klemeň	*stepbrothers, her*	*tenor*
Števa Buryja	*grandsons*	*tenor*
The Kostelnička *widow, her daughter-in-law*		*soprano*
Jenůfa *her foster-daughter*		*soprano*
The Foreman *at the mill*		*baritone*
The Mayor *of the village*		*bass*
The Mayor's wife		*mezzo-soprano*
Karolka *their daughter*		*mezzo-soprano*
A maid		*mezzo-soprano*
Barena *servant girl*		*soprano*
Jano *shepherd boy*		*soprano*
Aunt		*contralto*

Recruits, millworkers, servants

Helen Field as Jenůfa at Welsh National Opera (photo: Zoë Dominic)

Act One

Late afternoon. A lonely mill in the mountains. On the right, in front of the house. the overhanging roof is supported by wooden posts. Some baskets; some felled timber. In the background, a stream.

Scene One. *Jenůfa, a pot of rosemary in her hand, stands on a knoll by the stream and looks into the distance shading her eyes with her hand. Grandmother Buryja sits under the overhanging roof selecting potatoes from a basket, cutting their eyes out and throwing them into a bag. Left, on a tree trunk, sits dark-haired Laca whittling a whipstock.*

JENŮFA
(*to herself*)

Soon it will be evening and Števa has not come back;
terrible dreams have haunted me all through the night,
and dawn brought no rest but only new torments . . .
O Holy Mary,
if you do not hear my prayer,
if as a soldier my sweetheart is sent away,
so that we cannot be wed,
shame and dishonour will drive me to damnation!
O Holy Mary,
have mercy upon me!

Už se večer chýli a Števa se nevraci!
Hrůza se na mně věšala po celou noc,
a co jsem se rána dočkala, znova!
Ó Panno Maria,
jestlis mne oslyšela,
jestli mi frajera na vojnu sebrali
a svatbu překazili,
hanba mne dožene k zatraceni duše,
Ó Panno Maria,
buď' mi milostivá!

GRANDMOTHER BURYJA

Jenůfka, you're always leaving your work and running off!
Must I sit here and do all this work myself?
You know quite well these poor old eyes see very badly.

Jenůfka, pořád té od práce šidla honějí!
Mé ruce maji to všecko pokrájet?
Ke všemu na to staré oči špatně vidi.

LACA
(*ironically, sarcastic*)

Yes, Granny dear, yes, there are many things that you do not see;
you have always treated me just like any common labourer who must work to eat.
I'm not yours, that I know well,
not your flesh and blood.
You have gone out of your way to make me feel it;
after my parents had died, and I wanted affection,
when you fondled little Števa on your knee,
and stroked his fair hair,
and said it was 'golden just like the sun'
I was ignored by you, even though I too was an orphan. If you'd give me back my share . . .

Vy, stařenko, už tak na všelicos špatně vidite,
Nerobite ze mne vždycky jen člověka,
kterému se dáte najest, za to mládkovstvi najest?
Však já vim, že nejsem váš,
váš vlastni vnuk!
To jste mi pokaždé připamatovaly,
když jsem se chlapčisko siré za vámi přikrádal,
když jste mazlivaly Števu na klině,
a hladily jeho vlasy,
že 'žluté jak slunečko!'
Mne jste si nevšimly a já byl třeba také sirota. Kdybyste mi vyhodily . . .

JENŮFA
Kneeling, she turns away from the stream.

Laca, always speaking to poor Grandma so rudely!

Laco, vždy tak neuctivo k stařence mluviš!

43

Give back to me my twelve hundred crowns,
then I'd go away, go wherever I wanted!

... těch dvanáct set mého podílu,
mohl bych jít, kam by mne oči vedly!

JENŮFA

And you expect us to love you!

Potom tě mají mít rády!

GRANDMOTHER BURYJA

Truly, he behaves as though I don't matter.
Truly, he does not consider me mistress here,
nor as one of the family.

Baže, baže, jsem u něho jen výminkárka
Baže, nepovažuje mne za hospodyň,
natož za rodinu!

LACA
(to Grandmother Buryja)

And now you expect Jenůfa to work hard,
wondering if Števa's been conscripted.

A Jenůfu dnes voláte k práci,
když čeká Štefka od asenty?

JENŮFA
(to herself)

How well he knows what I am hiding in my heart!
Ah, how deeply those penetrating eyes can see into my heart!
I shall not even bother to answer him, wretched man.

On vidí člověku az do srdce
těma pronásledujícíma očima,
Ani mu odpovídat nebudu, zlochovi.

(to Grandmother Buryja)

Grandma, dear, do not be upset!
I'll make up for all the work I've missed.
I was afraid my rosemary plant would wither up and die:
that's why I ran off to water it.
If my plant should wither,
you know Grandma dear,
that saying,
that happiness and joy would wither also.

Stařenko, nehněvejte se,
já to všecko vynahradím.
Vzpomněla jsem si na rozmariju, že mi usychá,
šla jsem ji omočit k vodě.
A kdyby mi uschla,
viďte, stařenko, říká se,
že uschne potom
všechno štěstí v světě.

JANO
(calling from the mill)

Jenůfka, hey, Jenůfka, hey!
I can read now, now I know how to read.

Jenůfka, ej, Jenůfka, ej!
Už znám čítat, už jsem to potrefil!

(pleading)

Won't you write for me,
just a few more pages?

Narysajte mi
zase jiný listok!

JENŮFA

Patience, patience, Jano!
When I go to the town again, I'll bring you a reading book, and you can teach yourself then!
I shall teach you how to write as well, you'll be glad of that when you're older.
And now off to work with you,
or we'll have Grandma scolding us again!

Dočkaj, dočkaj, Jano!
Dočkaj až půjdu do města, přinesu ti čítanku, a v té si budeš říkat!
Aji psát tě, psat tě naučím, aby z tebe byl lepší člověk.
A včil si jdi po práci,
aby nás stařenka nehubovaly!

JANO
(distant, from the mill)

Hey, hey, hey, hey!
I know how to read,
Jenůfa has taught me to read!

Ej, ej, ej, ej!
Čitat umím, ej, čitat umím, ej.
Jenůfa mě naučily!

GRANDMOTHER BURYJA
(more mildly)

That is what you enjoy!

Co to máš za radost!

Yes, my girl, that is what you enjoy!	Co to máš, děvčico, za radost!
You've taught Barena to read and write already!	Barenu jsi naučila také čítat!
You've a man's common sense like your foster-mother,	Mužký rozum máš po svojí pěstounce,
there's no doubt at all you should have been a teacher.	učitelem, učitelem být si měla.

(*sighing*)

Ah! Yes;	Ba, ba,
but Granny dear,	můj rozum, milá stařenko,
my common sense has long ago flowed away like water in the mill stream.	už dávno mi tu někde do voděnky spadl.

Scene Two. *The Foreman in a suit, not overalls, whitened with flour, comes along and stops by Laca.*

THE FOREMAN

| What are you doing, Laca? | Co to robíš, mládku? |
| That's a fine whip-stock you have there. | Může být pěkne bičiště! |

LACA

| With such a blunt knife it will take me hours to get it finished. | Mám tupý křivak abych se s tím dvě hodiny páral! |
| Sharpen it for me! | Nabrus mi ho! |

THE FOREMAN
(*taking a whetstone from his pocket and sharpening the knife*)

| I'll sharpen it! | Nabrousím! |

Laca flicks Jenůfa's kerchief from her head with the end of the whipstock.

JENŮFA
(*without turning round*)

| Stop that Laca! | To ty, Laco, |
| You always want to plague and torment me ... | tys odjakživa takový divoň ... |

LACA

| If it had been Števa who had done that, then would you have minded? | Kdyby ti to Števa učinil, to by nevadilo? |

JENŮFA

| Števa would never do it. | On by to tak neučinil ... |

LACA

| Ah, then you would have minded? | Viď, to by nevadilo? |

JENŮFA

| Števa would never do it. | ... on by to tak neučinil. |

LACA

| Only because you are always standing so close together! | Protože vždy se mu hodně postavíš na blízko! |

JENŮFA

| That's not your business, | Co je ti po nás, |
| that does not concern you. | o sebe se starej! |

Jenůfa goes into the house by the porch; after a while she comes out again, settles herself by the basket and busies herself with the potatoes.

45

LACA

(to the Foreman who gazes after Jenůfa as she goes off)

She'll make a charming sister-in-law,
she'll be so kind and so good to me! . . .

To bude pěkná švagrina,
všeho mi dobrého nachystá!

FOREMAN

Yes, yes, she is lovely indeed;
she could turn your head completely;
she's as graceful as a flower,
and with those big dove-grey eyes of hers,

she tears the soul out of you.
She is lovely indeed, she could turn your
head completely.
But there's no need to tell you all this,
for you know yourself the power those
eyes have!

Což, což, což, pěkná je,
až se z toho hlava mate; což, pěkna je!
Nese se jak holba máku, jak holba máku,
a s těma sivyma očima by duši z těla
vytáhla.
Což, pěkná je!
Což, pěkná je, až se z toho hlava mate!

Ale nač tobě to vykládám,
však tys jejich oči také zkusil!

LACA

(scornfully)

I . . . I . . . You might well have seen just
how much I love her.
Just now she was grieving over her rosemary,
that was because she didn't know I'd put
worms all around the plant,
so that it, just like her wedding, would be
destroyed,
like this wedding she and Števa plan,
which they're both preparing for.

Ja, ja! Mohl jsi se přesvědčit, kterak ji
lubim,
Naříkala si tu nad rozmaryjou.
Netuší, že jsem ji do hliny zahrabal žižaky,

aby ji zrovna tak, zrovna tak povadla,

jak ta její svatba se Števkem,
ke ktere se chystají.

THE FOREMAN

See now, Laca,
that is what I find so strange.
with other people,
you behave as though you were a scoundrel.
Come, now,
you cannot tell me that you are really so
hard-hearted.
And I have often noticed
that when Jenůfa is here, you are different.

Vidíš, Laco,
to je mi podivné,
co z tebe robi
takového, takoveho zlocha,
Však ty nezapiraj,
nezapiraj, nemáš takoveho srdce.

A pozdává se mi,
že před Jenůfou měnivaš barvu.

LACA

Foolish talk!
That is nonsense.
Just remember,
remember she's not his yet,
for if today he has been conscripted,
there will be no wedding.

Hlupoty!
Běž si po svém!
Ale starku,
on ji ještě nemá, on ji ještě nema.
Jestli ho dnes při asentě odvedli,
bude po svatbě . . .

THE FOREMAN

He's not taken!
I met the messenger just now. Only nine
altogether were recruited, and Števa's
not taken!

Neodvedli! Neodvedli!
Potkal jsem poseláka; je jich odvedeno
všeho všudy devět — a Števa ne!

JENŮFA

(jumping up for joy)

He's not taken!

Neodvedli!

(kissing Grandmother Buryja)

God be praised, he's not taken, oh dearest
Grandma!

Bože můj, neodvedli! Stařenko moja!

LACA

He's not taken!

Neodvedli!

46

He's as strong as ten men! And they dare to call this justice!

To je potom spravedlnost! Šohaj jako skala!

GRANDMOTHER BURYJA

He's not taken!
Since he was a baby, Števa has always been lucky.

Neodvedli!
Už mu štěsti odjakživa přeje.

THE FOREMAN

He's not taken!
He's been lucky since he was a baby!

Neodvedli!
Už mu štěsti odjakživa přeje.

LACA

And they dare to call this justice!

To je potom spravedlnost!

Kostelnička enters.

KOSTELNIČKA

Števa's not been taken?

Števu neodvedli?

LACA

And they dare to call this justice!

To je potom spravedlnost!

JENUFA

Welcome, welcome, mamičko!

Vitajte, vitajte, mamičko!

Kostelnička enters the mill.

THE FOREMAN

Here, take it;
this knife of yours, I'm afraid,
just won't sharpen.

Na, křivak;
zdá se mi, že se nedá dobře brousit.

Scene Three. *The Foreman says goodbye and goes in.*

GRANDMOTHER BURYJA
(about to go in after Kostelnička)

Come now, Jenůfa, we must go and join your mother.

Co ty, Jenůfo, za mamičkou nevejděšěs?

JENUFA

Grandma, I beg of you — don't make me go in with mother!
Don't make me, Grandma!

Pro Boha, stařenko — neposilejte mne za ni!
Neposilejte!

GRANDMOTHER BURYJA

Child, you're acting so strangely!

Divna's, děvčico, divna's jaksi děvčico!

Scene Four. *The song of the recruits and the band playing is heard off stage.*

RECRUITS

They're all for marrying,
Rather than soldiering!
But I shall not be wed!
I'll join the army instead!
If I were rich I could buy myself out of it,
But I've no money to pay,
So I'm a soldier today.

Všeci sa ženija,
Vojny za bojija,
A já sa neženim,
Vojny sa sebojim!
Kery je bohatý, z vojny sa vyplati,
A já neboráček
Musim být vojáček.

STEVA

And so a-soldiering I must go!
And then there'll be no more courting!

A já tim vojákem musim být,
A já tim vojákem musim být!

JENŮFA
(looking around the recruits and recognising Števa)

Števa!   Števa!
Števuška!   Števuška!

RECRUITS

Then there'll be no more courting!   A konec milováni, a konec milováni,
Hi there! Hi there! Hi there!   Juchej! Juchej! Juchej!

Recruits enter from the left.

THE FOREMAN

Števa has brought the music with him!   Števa se nechá doprovázet!
You can all see now that he's not been   Poznat to na ném, že ho neodvedli!
taken!

Števa appears with the recruits and four musicians. Jenůfa goes to meet him.

RECRUITS, MILLWORKERS & SERVANTS

Hurrah there!   Ej, juchej! Ej, juchej!

RECRUITS

They're all for marrying,   Všeci sa ženija,
Rather than soldiering,   Vojny sa bojija,
But I shall not be wed.   A já sa neženim,
I'll join the army instead!   Vojny sa nebojim.
If I were rich I would buy myself out of it,   Kerý je bohatý, z vojny sa vyplati,
But I've no money to pay,   Z já neboráček
So I'm a soldier today.   Musim být vojáček.

LACA AND CHORUS

If they were rich they'd buy themselves out,   A bohatý z vojny sa vyplati,
Yes, they would buy themselves out.   Z vojny sa vyplati.

Števa, ginger blond, with a lock of hair combed over his forehead — drunk — unsteady on his legs, waves his flower-bedecked hat.

ŠTEVA

And so a soldiering I must go,   A já tim vojákem musim být —
Then there'll be no more courting!   a konec milovani, a konec milovani!

RECRUITS

Then there'll be no more courting!   A Konec milovani, a konec milovani!

JENŮFA

Števa!   Števo!
Števuschka! Števa!   Števuško! Števo!

Scene Five.

JENŮFA
(reproachfully)

My dear heart, my Števa, Števuschka!   Duša moja, Števo, Števusko!
Oh! Števa you're drunk again!   Tys zase už napilý?

ŠTEVA

I, I!   Já, já! Já, já!
You say I'm drunk?   Já napily?
This from you,   To ty mné Jenůfa?
Jenůfa?   Jenůfka?
Ah, you know my name is Štefan   Viš, že já se volám Štefan
Buryja?   Buryja?
That I'm owner of this mill?   Že mám půllánový mlýn?
That is the reason all the girls like me!   Proto se na me dévčata smějú!

48

(indicating the posy)

See this posy that I have here? That's from one of them!	Tuhle voničku jsem dostal od tej jednej.

(to the musicians)

Why have you stopped your playing?	Co nehrajete?
You underfed scrapers you!	Vy hladoví zajíci!

He throws money with both hands, which the musicians pick up.

Here, take it!	Tu máte!
Play the song that Jenůfa likes:	Zahrejte tu Jenůfčinu:
'Far away there in the town of Nové Zámky . . .'	'Daleko široko do těch Nových Zámkú . . .'

ŠTEVA, RECRUITS, MILLWORKERS, SERVANTS

Far away there in the town of Nové Zámky stood a high tower built of fine and handsome fellows.	Daleko, široko do těch Nových Zámkú; stavija tam vežu ze samých šohájkú.
High above all was a handsome young boy standing and his fair hair like a golden dome was shining.	Mojehu milého na sam vršek dali, zlatú makovénku z něhu udělali.
But the boy's sweetheart had seen this fine dome falling,	Zlatá makovénka dúle z veže spadla,
She was there waiting and in her lap caught it.	Moja galenečka do klina ju vzala.
Yes, she saw that golden dome was falling down and in her lap she caught it!	Moja galanečka zlatú makovénku, do klina ju vzala!

ŠTEVA

Come now, Jenůfa!	Pojď sem, Jenůfka!

ALL THE MEN

Yes, she saw that golden dome was falling down and in her lap she caught it!	Moja galanečka zlatú makovénku, do klina ju vzala!

Števa clasps Jenůfa round the waist.

ŠTEVA

So, we will dance to our wedding!	Tak půjdem na vdavky s muzikou!

Kostelnička stops the musicians with a gesture of the hand.

KOSTELNIČKA

So, this is the way your whole life would be, and you, Jenůfa, you would have to live on what was left after this spendthrift has wasted his money!	A tak bychom šli celým životem, a ty Jenůfa, mohla bys ty rozhazované peníze sbírat!
This whole family is the same!	Verná jste si rodina!
Ah, he too was so strong and manly, golden-haired and handsome; I longed for him to be mine even before his first marriage, even more after his wife died.	Aji on byl zlatohřivy a pěkně urostlý, že jsem po něm toužila, už než se poprvé oženil, aji za vdovca znova!
Mother had warned me against him, said that he'd always been a hopeless spendthrift!	Matka mi zbraňovala, že už se tehdy začal chytat světa!
I paid no heed to what she said.	Ale já neuposlechla!
Never once did I go home to complain of him, even when week after week he came back drunk; until in the end he was never sober at all! He got into debt, squandered every penny we had.	Ale po tom jsem si nešla postesknout, když se mí týden co týden opíjal, a posději chvíla co chvíla opíjal, dluhy robil, peníze rozhazoval!
Then when I tried to reason with him he beat me cruelly,	Počala jsem mu předhazovat, a tu mě bijával,

49

many a night I had to hide in the fields to escape from him! I have a feeling deep within me that the miller of Veborany is not yet worthy to be married to my foster-daughter.	že jsem mnoho nocí prožila po polích schovaná! Já už to dávno, dávno cítím, že třeba Veboranský mlynář, ještě není hoden státi vedle mojí pastorkyně!

JENŮFA

Mamičko, don't be angry.	Ó mamičko, nehněvejte se.

KOSTELNIČKA

I have said nothing to you until now because I know you love him. Tell him this: I will not give my permission for you two to marry yet, not till Števa's done a year's trial, during which he'll give up drinking.	Pořád jsem ještě, ještě mlčela, to tvému srdci kvůli! Pověz mu, že já nedovolím, abyste se prv sebrali, až po zkoušce jednoho roku, když se Števa neopije.

ALL THE MEN

How can she be so hard-hearted?	Ale je to přísná ženská!

KOSTELNIČKA

If you should disobey, Jenůfa, if you let yourself be influenced by Števa, God will surely strike you.	Neuposlechneš-li, Jenůfa, dáš-li jeho slovům přednost před mýma, Bůh tě tvrdě ztrestá!

GRANDMOTHER BURYJA

Oh stop, my daughter!	O dcera moja, dcera moja,

Števa, shaken, leans his head against the pillar.

She is so hard-hearted.	je to přísná ženská!

KOSTELNIČKA

You must go away tomorrow . . .	Zítra ihned dom mi půjdeš . . .

GRANDMOTHER BURYJA

But he's not really as bad as you think!	Vždyť on ten šohájek není tak zlý!

LACA
(ironically aside)

She keeps on spoiling him.	Pohlaďte šohájka, pohlaďte!

KOSTELNIČKA

Then there will be no more gossip that you only seek your fortune here.	. . . aby lidé neříkali, že se za tím Štěstím dereš.

LACA

Kostelnička, you have dropped your shawl, and I would also like to kiss your hand.	Kostelničko, upadl vám šátek! A já bych vám také, také ruku políbil.

ALL THE MEN

How can she be so hard-hearted?	Ale je to přísná ženská!

KOSTELNIČKA

I hope you all enjoy yourselves here!	Mívajte se tady dobře!

GRANDMOTHER BURYJA

Now then, all you fiddlers, get off home! Leave our lads alone now! Get off home!	A vy muzikanti jděte dom, jděte dom! Nesvádějte chlapců! Jděte dom!

ALL

Get off home! Now then all you fiddlers,	jděte dom, jděte dom, A vy muzikanti,

English	Czech
Get off home, Leave our lads alone now, Get off home, *etc.*	jděte dom, nesvádějte chlapců . . . jděte dom, *etc.*

| Get off home! | Jděte dom! |

GRANDMOTHER BURYJA

| Go and sleep now,Števuško,
Go!
You're young yet,
led on by your companions;
and you forget yourself! | Jdi se vyspat,Števusko
jdi!
Seš mladý,
kamarádi tě svadi,
zapomněl, zapomněl jsi se! |

RECRUITS

| Led on by your companions? | Kamarádi tě svádi? |

GRANDMOTHER BURYJA

| And you, Jenůfa, don't cry!
Love must always endeavour
over misfortune to triumph. | A ty Jenůfo, neplač, neplač!
Každý párek si musi svoje trápeni přestát,
svoje trápeni přestát — |

THE FOREMAN
(*then everyone*)

| Love must always endeavour,
over misfortune to triumph. | Každý párek si musi svoje trápeni přestát,
svoje trápeni přestát — |

All leave, except Jenůfa and Števa.

Scene Six.

JENŮFA
(*quietly, to Števa*)

| Števa,Števa, I know you got drunk today
because you were so happy.
But I beg you, Števuska,
don't make my mother cross;
You know my trouble,
I'm so afraid my heart trembles within me,
lest my mother and all the neighbours
find out about my guilty secret.
I dread the punishment that might fall on me;
all night long I lie awake.
And remember, my beloved,
God has only helped us over your conscription,
so that we might soon be married.
Even without that I shall be reproached
quite enough by my mother!
She has always been so proud of me, you know,
you have heard her.
I don't know
what I'd do if we did not get married in time!
I don't know
what would happen to me! | Števo,Števo, já vim, žes to urobil z té radosti dnes.
Ale jinda,Števuško,
nehněvej mamičku;
viš, jak jsem bédná!
Srdce mi úzkosťů v těle se třese,
že by mamička aj lidé mohli poznat moji vinu.
Bojim se, že na mne padne kdysi trest;
celé noci nespim.
Pamatuj se, duša moja,
když nám Pánbůh s tim odvodem včil pomohl,
abychom se mohli sebrat!
Bez toho bude od mamičky těch výčitek dost, dost!
Viš, jak si na mně zakládá,
včils ju měl slyšet!
nevim, nevim,
co bych udělala, kdybys ty mne včas nesebral,
nevim, nevim,
co bych udělala také já! |

ŠTEVA

| Do be quiet!
Now look here,
Aunt Kostelnička always scolds me
all for your sake,
and it's only because I love you; | Neškleb se,
vždyť vidiš,
tetka Kostelnička mne pro tebe dopaluje,
a to pro moji lásku k tobě, |

just now you could have seen it,
how all the girls are eager to smile at me.

Mohly byste se divat,
jak o mne všechna děvčata stoji!

JENŮFA
(*irritated*)

Yes, but now you should take no notice,
I am the one whom you belong to.
If you left me
I'd have to kill myself!

Ale včil na ně hledět nemáš,
Jen ja mám velké právo k tobě,

smrt bych si musela urobit!

(*seizing him by the shoulder*)

God! How can you behave like this?
So weak and foolish,
how can you let yourself be so foolish?

Ty mi takový nesmiš byt,
Bože můj,
slabý, směšný, takový, takový, takový
směšny!

(*shaking him*)

ŠTEVA
(*trying to calm Jenůfa*)

You don't really think that I'd leave you?
For your cheeks are like two rosy apples,
Jenůfa;
You are far the fairest of all creatures,
yes, you're far the fairest!

Však tě snad nenechám tak!
Už pro tvoje jablúčkový lice,
Jenůfo,
ty jsi věru ze všech nejpěknějši,
ty jsi ze všech nejkrásnějši!

JENŮFA

Ah! If you left me I'd kill myself!
If you left me, I'd have to kill myself!

Smrt bych si musela urobit!
Smrt bych si musela urobit!

GRANDMOTHER BURYJA

Come, stop this arguing!
His head will be much clearer in the
morning!
Go, Števa, go and lie down now!

O nechte hovorů,
až zitra, až bude mit čistou hlavu!

Běž, chlapče, běž si lehnout!

ŠTEVA

O Jenůfa!
You are far the fairest of all creatures!

O Jenůfa,
ty jsi ze všech nejkrásnějši,

Far the fairest . . .

(*going off*)

nejkrásnějši!

Grandmother Buryja and Števa go off. Jenůfa sits down once again by the basket with bowed head, and begins to work.

Scene Seven. *Laca gets up. He has thrown away the whip and has the knife in his hand.*

LACA

How all this boasting of Števa suddenly
faded, when Kostelnička scolded!

Jak rázem všecko to Števkovo vypináni
schliplo, schliplo před Kostelničkou uši!

JENŮFA

Even so, he remains a hundred times better
than you.

Přes to zůstane on stokrát, stokrát lepši než
ty!

LACA

Even now!

Zůstane!

Feverish with passion, he picks up the posy that was thrown away.

Jenůfa, here is the posy which he dropped
just now.
One which he was given by a girl,
by one of those whom he says, always smile
at him!
Look now!
I'll pin it there on your dress for you . . .

Jenůfa, tuhle mu upadla ta vonička,

co dostal od některé z těch,
co prý se na něho všude smějú!

Okaž,
já ti ji zastrčim za kordulku . . .

(drawing herself up proudly)

Give it to me!	Dej ji sem!
This little posy,	Takovou kytkou,
which my sweetheart was given to honour him,	kterou dostal můj frajer na počest,
I'll wear it proudly.	mohu se pýšit!

LACA
(aside)

You'd wear it proudly!	Budeš se ji pýšit.

(aloud)

And even though he sees nothing else in you,	A on na tobě nevidí nic jiného,
but those cheeks of yours like rosy apples.	jen ty tvoje jablučkové líca.

(with a glance at the knife in his hand)

Think how easily this knife could spoil those cheeks for you.	Tenhle křivák by ti je mohl pokazit.

Barena comes out to work. Laca approaches Jenůfa feverishly excited, holding the posy and the knife in his right hand.

But you're not going to get those flowers for nothing.	Ale zadarmo ti tu voničku nedám!

(trying to embrace her)

JENŮFA
(defending herself)

Laca, I shall hit you!	Laco, uhodím tě!

LAC

What have you got against me?	Co máš proti mně?

JENŮFA
(crying out)

Jesus Maria!	Ježiš, Maria!

As she defends herself, and as he is leaning down to her, he passes his knife across her cheek.

Laca — you have slashed my cheek!	Tys mi probodl lico!

She presses her scarf to her cheek. Barena raises her hands in horror.

LACA
(on his knees, holding Jenůfa in his arms)

What have I done to you?	Co jsem to urobil?
Jenůfka!	Jenůfka!

Jenůfa runs off into the building.

I have loved you all my life,	Já ťa lúbil, já ťa lúbil
All my life I've loved you!	od maličká . . .

GRANDMOTHER BURYJA
(hurrying out)

What's this?	Co to?
Whatever's happened?	Co se te děje?

THE FOREMAN
(hurrying out)

What's this?	Co to?
What is it?	Co to?
Whatever's happened?	Co se to děje?

BARENA
(urgently)

It was an accident,	Neštěsti se stalo,
they were fooling, he was only trying to kiss her.	laškovali o hubičku, o hubičku,
He had his knife in his hand like this	on si podržel křivák v ruce
and by accident, he scratched her cheek,	a tak, nechtěja, nechtěja
somehow scratched her.	ji poškrábl nějak lico.

The Foreman runs indoors after Jenůfa.

Thanks to heaven that it didn't go in her eye!

Zaplať Pánbůh, zaplať Pánbůh, že ji netrefil do oka!

GRANDMOTHER BURYJA

Only sorrow,
that is all you boys have ever brought me!

Samou žalost,
vyvádíte, vyvádíte chlapci!

THE FOREMAN
(returning)

Grandmother, come to Jenůfa!
She is fainting;
send someone for Kostelnička,
she must come here!

Stařenko, pojd'te k Jenůfě,
ona může z toho zamdlít!
Pošlete pro Kostelníčku,
at' jde hojit, honem hojit!

The grandmother hastens indoors. Laca pulls himself together and rushes off.

She can help her!

Honem hojit.

The foreman calls after him.

Laca, don't run away,
you did to her it on purpose!

Laco, neutíkej,
tys ji to urobil naschvál, naschvál!

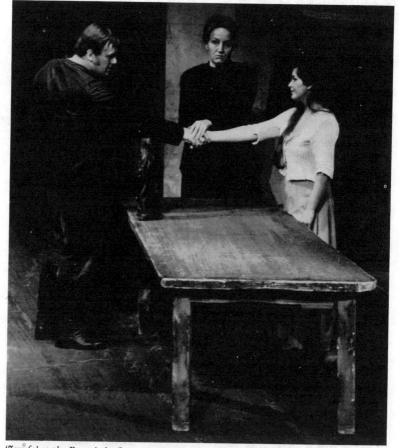

'Jenůfa' at the Bayerische Staatsoper, Munich in 1977; William Cochran as Laca, Joy McIntyre as Kostelnička and Gabriela Beňačová as Jenůfa (photo: Anne Kirchbach)

54

Act Two

Slovakian peasant living room, five months later. The walls covered with holy pictures and statuettes. By the door, a holy basin; elsewhere a stove, a feather bed made up for the day, a trunk (chest), a shelf with china, cutlery etc., a clothes chest; some chairs. By the window, a picture of the Virgin Mary.

Scene One. *Jenůfa is in ordinary peasant clothes, with an obvious scar on her palid cheek; she sits at the table sewing with bent head. Kostelnička goes to the side-door leading to the bedroom and opens it.*

KOSTELNIČKA

If I leave the door ajar a little,
then it will make your room warmer.
Tell me why you are always praying by the window
like a soul in torment?

Nechám ještě dveře otevřeny,
aby ti našlo dost tepla.
A co chodíš se k té okeničce modlit,

jako bludná duša?

JENŮFA

I cannot help it;
I have no peace of mind now!

Nemohu za to,
nemám, pokoje v hlavě.

KOSTELNIČKA
(*sighing*)

I believe you . . .
I too have no peace of mind.
You were so upset that day when I brought you back home.
I sensed that some great misfortune had befallen you.
And later when you told me, when you confessed your shame to me . . .
Then I thought that such disgrace would kill me.
Fearfully I kept you hidden in your dishonour,
until the day when the boy first saw the light,
and all the time his father,
that worthy fellow, did not care a rap!

To ti věřím,
aj já nemám pokoje!
Už od té chvíle, co jsem tě dovedla dom,

napadlo mi z tvého naříkání
neštěstí.
A když jsi se mi potom přiznala se svým pokleskem,
myslela jsem, že i mne to musí do hrobu sprovodit!
Schovávala jsem tě s tizkosťou v tvoji hanbě,
až do té chvíle, co chlapčok uviděl svět;

a jeho hodný otec
se ani ve snu o to nestará!

Jenůfa hurries to the bedroom door and looks in.

JENŮFA

Hush now! I think I heard little Števa crying.

Tuším, že sebou Števuška zahýbl!

KOSTELNIČKA

How you always spoil the baby!
It would be far better if you went down on your knees and prayed,
Prayed that God might take it from you.

Pořad se s tim děckem mažeš,
misto abys Pánaboha, Pánaboha prosila

by ti ulehčil od něho!

JENŮFA
(*returning to the table to work*)

Ah, no!
He's still asleep!
He sleeps so sweetly,
so quietly.

A ne . . .
spí tiše . . .
On je tak milý . . .
on je tak milý, milý, a tichúčký.

KOSTELNIČKA

Better if you went down on your knees and prayed,
prayed that God might take it from you.

. . . misto abys Pánaboha prosila,

by ti ulehčil od něho!

55

JENŮFA

All these eight days that he's been alive, never, never has he once cried!	Co je těch osm dní na světě, nikdy, nikdy nezaplakal!

KOSTELNIČKA

But he'll soon be howling, he will drive us mad. Ah! His very existence makes me mad! Ah! How proud I was of you. God in Heaven!	Ale bude bečat, bude domrzat, bude bečat, domrzat! Krve, rozumu mně to upiji! A já si na tobě tak zakládala, Bože můj! Bože můj!

Laying her work aside, Jenůfa gets up.

JENŮFA

Ah, I feel so faint, Mamička!	Tak je mi až mdlo, mamičko.

KOSTELNIČKA

Ah, how proud I was of you!	A já si na tobě tak zakládala.

JENŮFA

I'll go and rest now, Mamička!	Mamičko, půdju si lehnout.

Kostelnička takes a small pot from the stove and hands it to Jenůfa.

KOSTELNIČKA

Yes, but you must swallow some of this first, you'll find it will make you sleep much better. Your bed is ready, and I have lit a candle for you!	Ale prve si to všecko vypij, aby se ti v spánku ulehčilo. Ustláno již máš, kahánek jsem ti také rozžehla!

JENŮFA

Good night, mamička!	Dobrou, dobrou noc, mamičko!

Jenůfa drinks and goes slowly into the bedroom.

Scene Two.

KOSTELNIČKA
(shutting the door after Jenůfa)

Yes, in all these twenty weeks that I've kept the shutters tightly closed, that worthy fellow Števa has not shown his face here. Today, though, I have sent to tell him he must come! Then we shall settle it. And the baby, it is pale like Števa, and, like its father, it disgusts me!	Ba, ta tvoje okenička už přes dvacet neděl zabedněna, a ten tvůj hodný frajer nenašel k ní cesty. Jen dočkej, neviš, že jsem ho dnes pozvala; rozhodne se to, rozhodne. A to děcko, celý bleď och Števa, zrovna se mi tak protiví.

(desperate)

How I have prayed and fasted, prayed that the child might not be born — but it has all been quite useless, it's been born a week now, and seems to be quite strong and healthy. So I'm forced to sacrifice Jenůfa to that wretched Števa; and more than that, I must be humble too.	Co jsem se namodlila, co jsem se napostila, aby to světa nepoznalo. Ale všecko, všecko marno! Dýchá to už týden a k smrti se to nepodobá. Nezbývá mi než Jenůfu dát Števkovi k utrápeni; a ještě se mu musim pokořit.

(a noise at the door)

Here he is!	Už jde!

She locks the bedroom door and opens the main door. Števa enters.

Scene Three.

ŠTEVA
(*oppressed*)

Aunt Kostelnička, in the note you sent me	Tetko Kostelničko, poslala jste cedulku, kdyż nepřijdu,
you spoke of some great misfortune if I did not come!	ż se stane hrozné neštěsti!
Tell me why you wanted me.	Co mi chcete povědět?

Kostelnička points to the bedroom door. Števa hesitates.

KOSTELNIČKA

Come inside . . .	Vejdi dál . . .
Why hesitate?	Co váháš?

ŠTEVA

I am uneasy . . .	Mně je tak úzko . . .
Something is wrong with Jenůfa?	Stalo se něco Jenůfě?

KOSTELNIČKA

She has recovered, and the baby is well too.   Ona už okřala a dítě je zdrávo.

ŠTEVA

What, it's born already?   Už je na světe?

KOSTELNIČKA
(*with deep reproach*)

And you did not even bother coming here, did not ask, even.	A tys nedošel se ani podívat, ani pozeptat.

ŠTEVA

Even so, I've thought about it often.	Já si na to mnohokrát vzpomněl
I was really very sorry.	a mrzelo mne to dost.
But then I recalled how you mocked me, how you always seemed to want to persecute me.	A kdyż jste se na mne tak osápla, pronásledovat jste mne chtěla,
And I thought how Jenůfa's beauty had been spoiled,	a zrovna se Jenůfě krása pokazila,
I could not help myself.	nemohl, nemohl jsem za to.

KOSTELNIČKA

Well, come and see her!   Tož jenom vejdi!

ŠTEVA

I am frightened.	Já se bojím.
Is she inside then?	Ona tu čeka?

KOSTELNIČKA

Jenůfa's sleeping.   Jenůfa spi.

She opens the bedroom door.

ŠTEVA

When did she get back from Vienna then?   Dojela už z Vidně?

KOSTELNIČKA

She was hidden in there.	Tu se schovávala.
There now, go in and look at your baby son.	Tam se podívej na svoje dítě, chlapčok,
Like you, he's called Števa;	také Števa;
I myself have christened him.	sama jsem ho okřtila.

ŠTEVA

Oh, poor little mite.   O, chuďátko.

Yes, poor little mite!   Ba, chuďátko!

I will gladly support it,	Já budu na ně platit.
but no-one must be told that I'm the father!	Jen nerozhlašujte to, že je to moje!

But it's far worse!, far worse for Jenůfa!   Ale stokrát bědnější je Jenůfa!

With a spasmodic movement she grips his hand and pulls him to the door of the bedroom.

You must come and look at her too...	Podívej se také na ni,
At Jenůfa! What has this poor creature done to you,	na Jenůfu! Čím ti bědná duša ublížila,
that you've brought her to such dishonour?	žes ji uvrhnul do té hanby,
But surely you will help her now?	a včíl ji nechneš pomocí?
Just look now,	Vžyť přece vidiš,
he is your son, your baby.	že chlapčok žije,
And he is so like you!	je cely po tobě!
Come now, Števa!	Pojď se, Števo,
Come now and look at him!	přece naň podivat!
See how on my knees I'm forced to ask this of you.	Na kolenou toho se musim dožadovat.

(falling on her knees)

Števa, won't you take them both and make her your lawful wife?	Števo, seber si oba svatým zákonem.

Števa covers his face with his hands.

Ah, do not desert my foster-daughter,	Neopusti moji pastorkyňu,
My daughter, my only joy...	moji dceru radostnou,
Even if with you she should be unhappy,	ať si již s tebou snáši všechno neštěsti,
You must not leave her with this shame upon her and on my name too...	jenom ať v té hanbě nezůstane ona a moje jméno...
You're weeping?	Ty pláčeš?

She stands up and takes him by the hand.

You're weeping?	Ty pláčeš?
Come to them, Števa, in your arms take your own baby,	vezmi si svého chlapčoka na ruce,
Comfort Jenůfa!	potěš Jenůfu!

(slipping his hand away)

Aunt, your words would melt a heart of stone,	Tetuško, kameň by se ustrnul,
but I cannot marry her!	ale vzit si ji nemohu,
It would bring misfortune on us both.	bylo by to neštěsti nás obou.

Why on you both?   Proč také tvoje?

Because she made me frightened,	Proto, že se ji bojim,
For she used to be so sweet and gentle,	Ona bývala taková milá,
So bright and gay.	tak veselá.
But suddenly she began to alter before my eyes,	ale nejednou počala se měnit mně před očima,
she became like you with your gloom and severity.	byla na vás podobná, prudka a žalostná.
Then when I saw her after the enlistment,	Když jsem ji ráno po odvodě uhlidal,
when I saw her cheek so badly cut,	jak měla to lico rozťaté,
all my love for her disappeared,	všecka láska k ni mi odešla.
and you, also,	A vás, tetko,
(don't be cross if I speak quite frankly)	nehněvejte se za upřimnost,
make me feel frightened;	také se bojim.
for you seem to me to be so strange, terrible,	vy mi připadáte tak divná, strašná
like some horrible sorceress,	jako nějaká bosorka,

following me and plaguing me,	která by za mnou chodila
always trying to persecute me!	a mne pronásledovala!
Anyway, I'm now betrothed again,	Potem jsem už zrovna zasliben
I'm going to marry Karolka!	s tou rychtářovou Karolkou!
So it's finished, really finished!	Už je všemu konec!

KOSTELNIČKA

| Števa! | Števo! |

JENŮFA
(from her bedroom in her sleep)

| Mamičko, see a stone will crush me! | Mamičko, kámen na mne padá! |

Števa visibly shudders and runs out of the room.

KOSTELNIČKA

Can she be awake?	Obudila se?
No, in her sleep she was calling out!	To se jen ze spaní nazvedla
Števa came and saw it...	a Števa to viděl...
Once more she's sleeping.	Už znovu spí.

She shuts the door again quickly. With suppressed fury:

He ran off, wretched fellow!	Utekl, duša bidná!
Nor did he once go near the baby,	A k ditěti se nepřiblížil
and it's his own flesh and blood!	a vlastní to jeho krev!

(with utmost excitement)

Oh, I feel that I could kill this poor little baby,	Och, byla bych s to toho červika zničit
and throw it at his feet —	a hodit mu ho k nohám:
'There! There it is,	'Na, ty to máš, ty to máš,
You have it on your conscience!'	ty to máš na svědomí!

(beginning to think in a calmer way)

| What must I do? | Ale co včil? |

The house door opens. Laca enters unobserved.

| Who will save her now? | Kdo ji zachrání? |

LACA

| Look, it's me, Aunty! | To jsem já, tetko. |
| You know how I like to come and talk to you when I'm feeling lonely. | Vite, jak rád k vám chodim s vámi se potěsit! |

Scene Five.

LACA

But just now I saw someone else was here.	Ale viděl jsem vcházet šohaje.
It was Števa, I am certain.	Byl to Števa, poznal jsem ho.
What did he want?	Co tu hledal, co tu hledal?
Does it mean perhaps that Jenůfa's back?	Vrátila se snad Jenůfa?

KOSTELNIČKA

| Yes, she's back. | Vrátila. |

LACA

| And so she'll marry him now. | A bude přece jeho? |

KOSTELNIČKA

| No... She did not speak to him at all. | Ne... ona s nim nehovořila. |

LACA

Why won't you let me have her?	A mně ji dát,
For you've encouraged me to hope that one day,	jak jste mně vždycky, vždycky těšívaly,
it might turn out like that.	že se to může stát!
Oh, I will never leave her,	Och, nepopustim od ní, nepopustim,
not for all the world.	za nic na světě!

I have kept her all this time,	já ji po ten celý čas,
all this time hidden in there.	celý čas tu schovávala.
Just a week ago she had a baby, by Števa!	Ona před týdnem dostala chlapca s nim, se Števkem.

LACA

Aunt, is this the truth you tell me?	Tetko, to že by se stalo?
You're only testing me!	Vy mne jen zkoušite!

KOSTELNIČKA

God is my witness,	Jak Bůh nad námi,
that what I say to you is but the simple truth.	Čistou ti pravdu v te těžkosti povídám.

LACA

Oh, Aunt,	Och, tetko, och, tetko,
such a burden weighs upon me like a stone,	těžkost jste mi urobila,
like a heavy stone . . .	jak by mi do hlavy, kamenem . . .
And now do you expect me to take Števa's baby?	A ja bych si měl sevrat to Števkovo děcko?

Kostelnička crosses the room, holding her head in her hands.

KOSTELNIČKA

Laca, you must believe me,	Laco ó veru, veru,
That poor child no longer lives . . .	už ten chlapčok nežije . . .
it died!	Zemřel . . .

LACA

And does Števa know that?	On to Števa věděl?

KOSTELNIČKA

He knows. Bah! With him I'm finished!	Věděl. No, já už ho neznám,
I pray now for vengeance on him	jen pomstu bych na něho svolala, na jeho
throughout his miserable existence.	celý život!

(with increased feverishness)

Now go!	Teď běž,
And try to find out when they plan to marry.	jen běž, a dozvěd'se tam, kdy chystaji svatbu!
I must know about it.	Já to musim vědět —
Now go!	jen běž!

LACA

Yes I'll go,	Tož ano, tož ano.
I'll only be a moment.	Co chvíla budu tady.
	Exit.

Scene Five.

KOSTELNIČKA

One moment . . .	Co chvíla . . . co chvíla . . .
In that moment must I forfeit all my hopes	a já si mám zatim přejit celou věčnost,
Of eternity?	celé spaseni?
What if I took the baby somewhere far away?	Což kdybych raději ditě někam zavezla?
No . . .	Ne . . . ne . . .
For he would always be a burden,	Jen ono je na překážku,
An everlasting shame and dishonour!	a hanbu pro celý život!
Yet by such a deed I could save her . . .	Já bych tim ji život vykoupila . . .
And God,	A Pánbůh,
He knows how it would be if the baby stayed here . . .	on to nejlépe vi, jak to všecko stoji.

She takes a woollen shawl from a hook and wraps it round herself.

So to the Lord our God I'll send the boy . . .	Já Pánubohu chlapce zanesu . . .
It will be swifter and better!	Bude to kratší a lehčí!
Then when the Spring melts the ice away,	Do jara, než ledy odejdou,
there'll be no trace of him.	památky nebude.

| God will surely take him, | K Panubohu dojde, |
| He is too young to have sinned yet. | dokud to ničeho nevi. |

(in the highest excitement, her senses disordered)

| How they would taunt me, | To by se na mne, |
| how they would plague Jenůfa! | na Jenůfu sesypali! |

She doubles herself up like a hag and points her finger.

Just look at her,	Vidíte ji, vidíte ji,
Kostelnička!	
	vidíte ji, Kostelničku!

She slips quickly into the bedroom and returns with the child, which she has wrapped in a shawl.

| Sin-begotten ... just like his miserable | Z hříchu vzešel, věru i Števova bídná duša! |
| father, Števa. | |

Scene Six. *Kostelnička locks the door and hurries away. Jenůfa comes into the room.*

JENŮFA

Mamička, my head is heavy.	Mamičko, mám těžkou hlavu, mám, mám,
Oh, my head is heavy!	jako samý, samý kámen;
Help me!	pomozte. Kde jste mamička?
Oh, mamička!	Kde jste mamičko?

(looking slowly around her)

| This is mother's room. | To je její jizba. |

(rubbing her forehead)

| And I must remain in there hidden in my | Já zůstávám v komoře, musím se tam stále |
| little bedroom, | skrývat, |

(anxiously)

| So that no one sees me here. | ať mne nikdo nespatři, ať mne nikdo nespatři. |

Mother will reproach me bitterly,	Mamička mi pořád vyčítají,
Her words like daggers pierce my heart.	trním to bodá do duše!
Now it's evening,	Už je večer,
I can have the shutters open!	smím odbednit okeničky.
All is dark,	Všude tma, všude tma,
and the moon sheds its light on all poor people ...	jenom měsíček lidem záři
and thousands and thousands of stars ...	a plničko, plničko hvězd ...
and Števa still has not come,	A Števa ještě nejde,
and now he will not come.	a zase nedojde!
If he could see his baby,	Kdyby tak chlapčoka viděl,
just see those deep blue eyes of his ...	jak modré oči otvirá ...
And where is my Števuska?	A kde je můj Števuška?
Where have you put him?	Kam jste mi ho daly?

She runs into the bedroom and comes back again.

| Where have you put him? | Kam jste mi ho daly? |

She searches among the bedding.

Where is my Števuska?	Kde je můj Števuška?
Ah, I can hear him,	Pláče a naříká,
I can hear him crying.	já ho přece slyším.
Do not hurt my baby, good people;	Neubližujte mu, dobři lidé,
I, and I alone am guilty:	já to všechno zavinila,
I and Števa.	já a Števa.
Where have you put my baby?	Kam jste mi ho položili,
Ah! He is falling!	spadne tam, ach, spadne.
He will catch cold there!	Zima mu bude, zima ukrutná!
Do not abandon him!	neopúštějte ho!

(crying out)

| Ah! Wait! | Dočkajte! |
| I will protect him! | Já ho přijdu bránit ... |

She runs to the door, which is locked, and presses against it with her hands. Quietly:

Where am I?	Kde to jsem?
Surely this is my mother's room ...	To je maminčina jizba,
And the door is locked ...	dvéře zamknuty, dvéře zamknuty,

Now I know, Mother has gone to the mill with him!	Že ho šly mamička ukázat do mlýna?
That's it . . .	Aha, aha, do mlýna,
She is showing them Števa's baby,	Števova synka,
Števa's baby!	Števova synka!

(worried)

But now I must pray for Števuška,	Ale modlit se musim za něho
kneeling here at the Holy Virgin's feet.	tam u mariánského obrázku.

She takes the picture from the wall, puts it on the table and kneels down.

Hail to Thee, Holy Queen,	Zdrávas královno,
Hail, Thou mother of mercy,	matko milosrdenství,
Hail, Thou our life and hope,	živote sladkosti,
Our hope and sweetness!	tys naděje naše!
All hail!	Buď zdráva,
All hail to Thee!	buď zdráva,
We call for help,	my k tobě voláme,
suffering, sorrowing children,	vyhnaní synové Evy,
to Thee we send our sighs, mourning and weeping	k tobě vzdycháme, lkajíci a plačíci
in this vale of tears.	v tomto slzavém údolí.
Oh, turn then, most gracious advocate,	Ach, obrať k nám své milosrdné oči,
Thine eyes of mercy towards us, and show us Jesus.	a Ježíše, který jest plod života tvého,
He is the blessed fruit of Thy womb,	nám po tomto putování ukaž,
after this our exile,	ó milostivá, ó přívětivá,
have mercy on us,	ó přesladká Panno Maria,
O most sweet Virgin Mary!	ó přesladká Panno Maria!

There is a noise at the door. Feverishly:

And Števuška protect for me,	A Števušku mi ochraňuj,
please do not forsake him,	a neopúšťaj mi ho,

(knocking at the door)

please do not forsake him,	neopúšťaj mi ho,
O most merciful mother!	matko milosrdenství!

Scene Seven. *Jenůfa jumps up.*

JENŮFA

Who is there?	Kdo to je?

KOSTELNIČKA
(from outside, distraught, panting and trembling)

Jenůfka,	Jenůfko,
You are still awake then?	ty jsi ještě vzhůry?
Open the window!	Otevři okno!

Jenůfa gently opens the window.

JENŮFA

Have you brought Števuska?	Nesete Števušku?

KOSTELNIČKA
(at the window, in a state of shock)

Quickly now, open the door for me.	Tu máš klíč, otevři, otevři dveře,
How my hands are trembling,	ruce se mi třesou . . .
frozen . . . frozen . . .	zimou . . . zimou . . .

Jenůfa shuts the window, but not completely — goes to the door and unlocks it.

JENŮFA

Where is Števuška?	Kde je Števuška?
Have you left him behind at the mill?	Vy jste ho nechaly ve mlýně?

(joyfully)

Mother, perhaps now Števa himself will come and bring his son with him, for he's such a lovely baby.	Snad k nám dojde sám Števa na besudu, viď te, mamičko, pro to roztomilé děcko?

Girl, these are delusions,	Děvčico, ty blouzniš.
God in Heaven help you!	Poteš tě Pánbůh!
But now I must tell you what has happened.	Ale ty ještě o tom neštěti neviš.
Two days you lay there in a fever,	Dva dny jsi spala v horečce,
and your poor baby died, it died!	A ten tvůj chlapčok umřel, umřel, umřel!

Jenůfa sinks down on her knees before Kostelnička and leans her head on her lap.

He died then,	Tož umřel, tož umřel,
my darling baby boy,	můj chlapčok radostný,
(sobbing)	
Mamička, how my heart is aching,	Mamičko, srdce mi boli,
though I know you always said to me	ale vy jste vždycky řikávaly,
that this would be the best thing for him,	že by mu to bylo k přáni,
for God could give him so much more,	že co mu Pánbůh nachystá,
more than I could offer him!	já bych bědna nemohla!
So my child died,	Tož už mi umřel,
now he's an angel in heaven.	tož je už andělíčkem,
But without him I feel so lonely,	ale já jsem tak sirá
I could weep.	bez něho, tak je mi těžko ...

You should give thanks to Heaven!	Poděkuj Pánubohu! Poděkuj, Pánubohu!
Now you are free again.	jsi zase svobodná!

(decisively, firm)

What of Števa?	A což Števa?
Mamička, you gave me your promise that	Mamičko, slibovaly jste mi, že pro něho
you would send for him.	pošlete.
We must tell him what has happened.	Ten to musí také vědět.

Put him from your mind;	Nevzpominej ho,
May his name be accursed!	leda kletbu mu přej!
He came here while you were lying	Byl tady, když jsi ležela v tom spánku,
sleeping,	
saw the baby,	dítě viděl,
then I went down on my knees before him,	já před něho na kolena padla,
but he offered money as recompense,	ale on to všechno chtěl zaplatit,
said you made him frightened,	Tebe že se boji,
said that your cheek was badly disfigured,	že máš to lico pošramocené,
said that I too frightened him,	mne se také boji,
like a sorceress, a sorceress!	že jsem bosorka, bosorka!

Oh, God forgive him!	Ach, Pánbůh mu odpust'.

Now he says he's going to marry Karolka!	A s tou rychtářovou už je zasliben.
Do not break your heart over this	Nelámej si pro tu slotu opijavého hlavu!
miserable drunken spendthrift!	
You should think rather of Laca!	A važ si raději Laci!
There you have a love you could depend on!	To máš pravou spolehlivou lásku!

Scene Eight.

He's coming now! ...	Tot'zrovna jde!
(to Jenůfa hurriedly)	
He knows all about it,	On o tobě všechno ví,
I have told him everything	já mu všechno pověděla,
and he forgave you.	a on ti odpustil, odpustil.

LACA

Aunty, Aunty,	Tetuško, tetuško,
no one was in at the Mayor's house.	nebyli u rychtářů doma.

He sees Jenůfa, and offers his hand.

Jenůfa!	Jenůfka!
God be with you,	Potěš tě Pánbůh,
Jenůfka!	Jenůfka!
Won't you give me your hand now?	Nepodáš mi ruky?

JENŮFA

I must thank you, Laca,	Děkuji ti, Laco,
for all your kindness,	za všecko dobré
and for the generous way in which you behaved	co jsi se o mně namyslel po ten čas,
while I was kept in hiding,	co jsem ti byla s očí!
I often sat in here and heard you talking,	Já jsem tě mnohokrát z komůrky slyšela,
heard how you always spoke of me with my dear mother.	jak jste tu s maničkou vždy o mně hovořili.
You know how I have suffered.	O vidíš, jak jsem bědná!

LACA

Soon you will be well again,	Však zase okřeješ,
and learn to bear your loss!	své dítě oželíš!

JENŮFA

I had never thought my life would be like this,	Já jsem si ten život jinak myslela,
never be like this,	jinak myslela,
but now I feel that this must be the end!	ale včil už jak bych stála u konce!

LACA
(sadly)

You mean that you will not take me	A za mne bys nešla,
Jenůfa, dearest Jenůfa?	za mne, Jenůfka?

KOSTELNIČKA

Yes, she'll take you, Laca,	Půjde za tebe, půjde, Laco,
she will take you!	půjde!
She's already come back to her senses,	Ona včil už ztracený rozum našla,

(sinking into an armchair)

and she must be happy once again.	a musí být ještě šťastná.

JENŮFA

Mamička talks sometimes so childishly!	Mamička tak dětinsky hovoří!
How could you marry me?	Jak by sis mne to vzal?
Oh, think it over, Laca!	O rozvaž si to dobře!
For I have neither wealth nor honour,	Majetku, počestnosti nemám,
and I could not offer the flower of my first love —	a lásky, té pěkné, pro všecko na světě,
that is gone for ever.	té už také nemám.
Do you want me like this?	Chceš mě takovou?

LACA
(taking her in his arms and kissing her on the cheek)

Yes, Jenůfka, yes,	Chci, Jenůfka, chci!
Jenůfka.	Jenůfka,

JENŮFA
(gently, lightly)

Then I will gladly share with you all the	Pak budu s tebou, s tebou snášet
good and all the ill that may befall us!	všechno dobré, všechno, všechno zlé!

LACA

If only you will take me!	jen když budeš, budeš má!

KOSTELNIČKA
(pulling herself up with an effort and going over to them)

Now, you see,
I have arranged it well;
Everything's all right now.
So receive my blessing
from a heart that is heavy.
May the Lord guide you safely
through all misfortune,
May He bless you with health,
with contentment and prosperity . . .
As for Števa,
he who is the cause of this misfortune
him I curse!
Should he wish to marry,
should he ever find a girl to take him,
better she should go mad before she
    crosses his threshold!
Woe to him and me!

Vidíte,
že jsem to přece dobře učinila,
dobře učinila, dobře!
A já vám včil žehnám
z toho těžkého srdce:
ať vás Panbůh vždy vytrhne
z každého trápení, z každého trápení,
ať vám žehná vždy na zdraví,
spokojenosti i majetku . . .
ale jemu,
té příčině všeho neštěstí,
kletbuju, kletbuju,
aby jeho žena,
která si ho s takým srdcem vezme,
spíše rozumu pozbyla, než překročí jeho
    práh!
Běda jemu i mně!

A draught forces the window open.

LACA

What is wrong, Aunty?

Co je vám, tetuško?

KOSTELNIČKA

Don't you hear outside there that wild
    lament?

Co to venku hučí, naříká?

(shrieks)

Hold me!

Držte mne!

Laca sympathetically puts his arm around her shoulders.

Do not leave me!
Laco, stay!

Stůjte při mně!
Laco, zůstaň!

She looks fearfully round her.

LACA

What is wrong, Aunty?

Co je vám, tetuško?

KOSTELNIČKA

Shut that window!

Zavřete okno!

Jenůfa goes to close the window.

JENŮFA

Ah, how bitter and cruel the wind!

Ha, jaký to vítr a mráz!

KOSTELNIČKA

The icy voice of death forcing his way in!

Jako by sem smrt načuhovala!

Act Three

Kostelnička's room as in Act Two. On the table, which is covered with a white cloth, stands the potted rosemary and a plate with a few rosemary sprigs tied up with a ribbon; a bottle of wine, glasses, a plate of small round cakes.

Scene One. *Jenůfa, in her best clothes, sits on a chair with a prayer book and a handkerchief in her hand. Laca stands near Jenůfa. Grandmother Buryja sits in an armchair by the table. Kostelnička walks up and down in feverish restlessness — she looks very pale and exhausted. Jenůfa seems more cheerful than in Act Two, but very serious.*

<table>
<tr><td colspan="2" align="center">MAID</td></tr>
<tr><td>Don't you feel nervous, Jenůfka?</td><td>Neni ti teskno, Jenůfko?</td></tr>
<tr><td colspan="2" align="center">JENŮFA</td></tr>
<tr><td>No, no!</td><td>Neni.</td></tr>
<tr><td colspan="2" align="center">LACA</td></tr>
<tr><td>Why should she be nervous?
She knows that I'll never harm her again.</td><td>Proč by ji bylo tesklivo,
však já ji jakživ neublížim?</td></tr>
<tr><td colspan="2" align="center">MAID</td></tr>
<tr><td>Well, that's what usually happens;
girls are sad when they lose their freedom.
God knows I was very stupid,
spent the whole time weeping.
Why, I can't imagine,
for I had married a good and honest man!</td><td>To už tak ale bývá,
že je děvčici lito svobody.
Bože, co já byla hlupa.
já se naplakala,
a zatim dostala jsem
dobrého, hodného, řádného člověka!</td></tr>
<tr><td colspan="2" align="center">KOSTELNIČKA
(frightened, shocked)</td></tr>
<tr><td>Who's that making a noise out there?
Who is there?</td><td>Co to šramoce za dveřmi?
Kdo to jde?</td></tr>
<tr><td colspan="2" align="center">MAID
(opening the door to the new arrivals)</td></tr>
<tr><td>Welcome!</td><td>Vitajte!</td></tr>
<tr><td colspan="2" align="center">(to Kostelnička)</td></tr>
<tr><td>Do not be afraid,
for it is only the Mayor and his wife.</td><td>Nelekejte se,
to je rychtař s rychtařkou.</td></tr>
</table>

Scene Two.

<table>
<tr><td colspan="2" align="center">MAYOR
(offering his hand to Kostelnička)</td></tr>
<tr><td>God be with you!
Were you afraid, frightened of us?
Us? Frightened of us?
You invited us to come.</td><td>Dej Bůh štěsti . . .
Což jste se nás polekala . . .
. . . nás polekala?
Došli jsme na pozvanou.</td></tr>
<tr><td colspan="2" align="center">MAID</td></tr>
<tr><td>That is just her illness.
Welcome! Welcome!</td><td>To je jeji nemoc.
Vitajte! Vitajte!</td></tr>
<tr><td colspan="2" align="center">MAYOR</td></tr>
<tr><td>Karolka's waiting for Števa,
they'll be here together.</td><td>Karolka jen co se dočká Števy,
Přijdou spolu.</td></tr>
<tr><td colspan="2" align="center">LACA</td></tr>
<tr><td>I bid you welcome!</td><td>Zdrávi došli.</td></tr>
</table>

JENŮFA

Welcome!

Vitajte!

MAID
(aside, at the table)

What is best for me to do now?
Should I give them flowers first or offer
them a glass of wine?
I have only come to help out.
Kostelnička is not quite herself yet after
her illness!

Nevím co se patří spíše,
či přišpendlit rozmaryju, nebo podat na
zavdanou.
Já jsem tu dnes na pomahaj.
Kostelnička je pořad po nemoci slabého
ducha.

She pours out the drinks and distributes the sprigs of rosemary.

MAYOR

Clearly she's failing,
one can see that!
I can remember how fit and strong you
were,
so alive and active!

Vidět to po ní, hyne,
hyne jaksi!
Co jste vy bývala za ženskou statečnou.

jen na vás všecko hrálo!

(raises his glass to her)

Here's an end to your troubles,
God grant you'll be well again!

At' už nenařikáte,
at' je všecko v pořádku!

KOSTELNIČKA

Today I've been preparing for Jenůfa's
wedding
with a worthy man;
that is no cause for weeping.
but I feel myself failing.

Vypravuju dnes Jenůfě svatbu s hodným
člověkem,

mně není do nářku.
Ale cítím to, hynu, hynu.

(clasps her head in her hands)

Ah, this unending torture!
Sleep cannot relieve the torment!
I must lie awake the whole night lest I be
spared a moment of it.

Och, bývají to muka!
Spanek nikdy neodlehčí,
musím být vzhůru, musím, abych to
všechno zažila.

JENŮFA

Mamička,
with the help of God above you'll soon
recover!

Mamičko,
však da Pánbůh, že se ještě uzdravíte!

KOSTELNIČKA

But I don't want that.
No!
I don't want that ...
Long life for me would only be torture,
only torture ...
and what then?

Nechci se uzdravit,
nechci,
nechci, nechci ...
Dlouhý život byl by hrůzou,
byl by hrůzou ...
a jak tam?

(pulling herself together)

This is your wedding day,
Jenůfa,
and that makes me happy.

Dnes je tvá veselka,
Jenůfko,
já se z ní těším.

MAYOR'S WIFE

What has given Jenůfa this strange idea,
that her dress is so plain and sombre on
her wedding morning?

Co si to jen Jenůfa vzala do hlavy,
že jde ke zdávkám jako mudrá vdova
nastrojená?

KOSTELNIČKA

What, Jenůfa?
All the finest gentry dress plainly and
simply when they go to the altar.
Why should my foster-daughter ignore the
fashion on her wedding day?

Ona, Jenůfa?
Zrovna tak jednoducho chodívají ku
oltáři největší páni.
Co by jen na obyčejno nastrojená nemohla
jít Jenůfa?

Gentry folk have their own fashions and customs, but we are only simple people, I'd never dream of being wed without my bridal crown and ribbons. Never, not for all the money in the world. Never!	Páni si dělají všecko po módách, ale my tady na dědině! No, já bych ku oltáři byla nešla bez věnce a pantli, ani za tisíc rýnských nešla, nešla!

KOSTELNIČKA

Come along and look at the trousseau I've made for her!	Pojďte se podívat na její výbavku!

MAID

Even so, Jenůfa will make a good and loving wife for Laca.	Proto ona přece zůstane spořádaná aj šikovná ženská!

KOSTELNIČKA

I have done it all, every stitch of it ... Such a fine trousseau you won't see every day!	Sama jsem já všechno, všechno spořádala. Takovou výbavku hned tak nevidět!

Everyone goes into the bedroom except Jenůfa and Laca.

Scene Three.

JENŮFA

There now, Laca, just as I foresaw, everyone was commenting on the way I'm dressed for my wedding.	Vidiš, Laco, já to tušila, že to každému napadne, jak jsem to na sdavky nastrojena.

LACA
(taking a little posy from his jacket pocket.)

Jenůfka, I at least have brought you these flowers ... They're from Belovce, from the old gardener.	Jenůfka já ti přece kytičku donesl ... Je až z Belovce od zahradníka.

JENŮFA

Thank you so much, Laca!	Děkuji ti Laco!

LACA

Won't you take them then? Jenůfka!	Tu bys nevzala, tu bys navzala? Jenůfka!

JENŮFA
(fastening the posy in her dress)

Ah, Laca! Truly you have not deserved such a bride.	Och Laco, takové nevěsty ty sis nezasloužil, nezasloužil!

LACA

Childish creature, don't say any more now! Only when Kostelnička told me, in that first moment I thought that I could never bear it! But then afterwards I could not help forgiving you! Ah, but I have sinned so deeply against you. My whole life I'll spend trying to make it up to you.	Ó dětino, už mi o tom nemluv! Mne jen to ranou udeřilo v tu první chvíli, jak mi to tetička řekely, ale potom hned jsem ti to odpustil! Však se já na tobě tak mnoho provinil. celý život tobě to musím vynahrażovat.

Laca, I feel so sorry,
in my misfortune you stood by me,
you, not Števa.

Tak mi je lito tebe, tak mi lito tebe!
Tys při mně stál v neštěsti,
ty, misto Števa!

LACA

I know that you loved Števa once,
if you could only not think of him!
My heart was full of hatred for Števa,
and I would have liked nothing better than
to ruin him.
But then you insisted that I should make it
up with him.
Now I've overcome all the evil in my heart,
All! For you are here with me,
therefore I thought it would be fitting if I
invited Števa to come here for our
wedding;
so as a brother he will come here with
Karolka.

Já vim, žes Števu lubila,
jenom když včil už naň nemysliš.
Já nosil v srdci zášť na Števu!
A o všechno bych ho byl nejraději připravil.

Ale tys mi nakázala, abych se s nim udobřil.

Já už jsem to všechno zlé v sobě překonal,
Všechno, že tys se mnou, že tys se mnou!
Števu jsem, jak se patři, pozval na naši
svatbu.

Slibil, že dojde jako bratr i s Karolkou.

Scene Four.

LACA

Aha! Here they are.

A hen ... už jsou tu!

Karolka and Števa enter.

KAROLKA

God be with you one and all.
Števa seemed to take so long in getting
ready,
that I thought his legs must have been
rooted to the floor!
My best wishes.
May you both be very happy, and may God
bless you both.
Watching you today will make me sad, and
envious too,
since it will be my turn soon to walk to the
altar.
It's really a shame though,
that it's such a simple wedding;
neither music nor a party!
Now then, Števa, your good wishes.

Pánbůh rač dát dobrý den, dobrý den!
Števa se tak dlouho zdržel se strojenim,

jako kdyby se mu nohy k zemi lepily!

Vinšuju vám, vinšuju vám,
aby vám dal Pánbůh štěsti.

Já se budu dnes na tebe skormoucené divat,

že to také na mne dojde jit ku oltáři

Jen škoda, jen škoda,
že si to tak jako mudři
bez muziky obdýváte!
A včil, Števo, vinšuj ty!

ŠTEVA

I can't speak half as well as Karolka!

Já to neumim jako Karolka!

JENŮFA

Well, never mind,
just come and shake hands with your
brother!
Each of you has something good to
recommend him.
You, Števa, you're handsome;
and Laca, you are so noble-hearted!

No neškodi,
tu podejte si s bratrem ruce!

Každý z vás má něco pěkného na sobě.

Ty, Števo, svou tvářnost,
a Laca tu dobrou boži duši!

KAROLKA

Oh, how I wish you wouldn't keep telling
him that he's handsome; for he's conceited
enough already!

Jenom ty ještě Števovi napověz,
že je pěkný;
bez toho nevi, co vyvádět!

JENŮFA

Surely he's outgrown all that by now?

Taký dětina on by ještě byl?

And how long must you wait till your wedding?

Kdy vy budete mit veselí?

Just two weeks from today.

Zrovna za čtrnáct dni.

(joking)

Ha, only if I feel like it!
I still have time to change my mind.
You should hear the warnings that I've had about you!

I ha, budu-li já jenom chtít!
Třeba tě ještě odpravím.
Bez toho mne lidé strašejú s tebou!

Ah! If you changed your mind,
I would have to kill myself!

Ty bys to dopravila,
život bych si musel vzít!

See now, Števa,
now you know what real love is!
May it never hurt you,
never turn to pain.

Vidiš, Števo,
to je tvoje pravá láska!
Bodajt' by tě nikdy nezabolela,
nezabolela!

The Mayor, Kostelnička and the others come in once more.

Scene Five.

There's no denying that all that was really a sight worth seeing.

To bylo ňákého, to bylo ňákého prohliženi!

(frightened, shocked)

Števa is here!
Has he come once more to bring misfortune here?

Števa je tu!
Došel zas urobit nějaké neštěti!

(to Laca)

Even though you beg me,
I just cannot bear to see him!

Uprosili jste mne,
ale nemohu ho vidět!

It's just as well I lit a cigar in there;
all that rummaging
would have made me furious!

Kdybych si nebyl zapálil cigárku,
už by to hrabáni mne bylo dopálilo!

(to Kostelnička)

But Jenůfa asked him, Jenůfa herself!

Když Jenůfa toho se dožadovala!

Well, she has a lovely trousseau,
you might well be proud of it!

Řádně jste ji vybavila, ta čest se vám musí dát!

Scene Six. *Barena and the girls enter with a posy tied with coloured ribbons.*

God be with you one and all!

Pán Bůh rač dát dobrý den!

We were not invited, but you
need not fear that we shall keep
you long. God be with you one and all!

Pan Bůh rač dát dobrý den!
Nepozvali jste nas, my vá
dlouho zabavovat nebudem.

BARENA

We all knew that there would be
no celebration, yet we had to
come here all the same, just to
sing our song to Jenůfa and to
give her our best wishes!

Bar zádného veseli nestrojite,
přece jsme se zdržet nemohly,
abychom nešly Jenůfě vinšovat
a zazpivat!

PEASANT GIRLS AND BARENA

We all wish you this: May you
have as many hours of joy as
there are stars in heaven!
And now we'll sing for you!

Tož vám oběma vinšujeme tolik
štěsti, co je kapek v hustém
dešti.
A teď' si zazpiváme!

Hey, mother, mother, little mother mine!
You must give me fine new clothes now,
For I shall be married today,
Hey!

Ej, mamko, mamko, mamènko moja!
Zjednejte mi nové šaty,
já se budu vydávati.
Ej!

Hey, daughter, daughter, little daughter
mine!
You are far too young to marry,
You must put such thoughts away.
Hey!

Ej, dcerko, dcerko, dceruško moja!
Nechaj toho vydávaňa,
však si ešče hrubé mladá.
Ej!

Hey, mother, mother, little mother mine!
Don't forget that you were young once,
So let me be married today.
Hey!

Ej, mamko, mamko, mamñenko moja!
Také vy jste mladá byly,
ráda jste se vydávaly.
Ej!

MAYOR

Well, you sang that very nicely, charming.

Dobře jste to zazpivaly, dobře, dobře,
dobře!

BARENA
(giving Jenůfa a posy)

And then we've brought you these, Jenůfa!

A to si od nás vezmi, Jenůfko!

JENŮFA

Thank you, thank you all, I cannot
tell you how deeply it has touched
me!

Děkuju, děkuju vám z celého srdce!
Tak mile mne to dojalo!

LACA

The Preacher said that we must be
at church at nine o'clock exactly.

Pan farář nakázali přijit do
kostela zrovna v devět!

MAYOR

Well, we must hurry, but first the
blessings, so that we can go!

Tož si jen popilte s požehnánim,
aby už to šlo!

Laca and Jenůfa kneel down before Grandmother Buryja

GRANDMOTHER BURYJA

So now I bless you, in the name
of the Father, the Son, and the
Holy Spirit.
Laca, don't think badly of me!

Tož já vám žehnám, ve jmenü
Otce, Syna aj Ducha svatého.

Ty, Laco, men sle nevzpominej!

The bride and groom kiss the hand of Grandmother Buryja.

MAYOR

Now you, Kostelnička, you should
know the way to do it as the
priest would do it.

A včil, Kostelničko, vy
to asi dokážete jak velebníček!

The bride and groom kneel before Kostelnička; she raises her hand. There is a noise outside.
Kostelnička draws back in horror. Two voices are distinguished from outside.

Poor baby!	Chuďátko!
Oh, what a monstrous thing,	Nějaka bestyja uničila
murdering a baby!	dité!
What ungodly wretch could have	Kera bezbožnica to
killed a baby?	urobila?

KOSTELNIČKA

What baby?	Co dité?

Scene Seven.

KOSTELNIČKA

What baby's that they're shouting about?	Co s ditětem tam kričji?

JANO
(*rushing in*)

Where's the Mayor?	Ruchtaři,
You must come!	hledaji vás!

MAYOR

What's happened? What is it?	A co je? A co je?

JANO

Don't you know what's happened?	Vy to jeśtě nevite?

ŠTEVA

What has happened?	Co se děje?

JANO

Men from the brewery found it	Sekáčiz pivovaru naśli pod ledem
under the ice, a frozen baby!	přimrzle dité!

CHORUS

Oh horror! Oh horror! Oh horror!	Ó hrůza! Ó hrůza! Ó hrůza!

JANO

As they held it,	Nesou ho na desce,
it seemed like a live baby lying there,	je jako živé v peřince,
wrapped up tightly,	v povijáku, na hlavě červenou pupinu.
wearing a little red cap on its head.	To je na hrůzu, to je na hrůzu;
Oh, it was awful!	lidé nad tim nařikaji.
Out there everyone is weeping!	nad tim nařikaji.

Scene Eight.

JANO

Come quickly now!	Ó poběžte!

Jano runs out, followed by the Mayor, his wife, the maid, Laca, Jenůfa and Karolka. Only Steva remains standing as if petrified. Kostelnička stays by the bed; near her, Grandmother Buryja.

KOSTELNIČKA

Jenůfa,	Jenůfa ...
don't go out there!	... neodbihaj,
Hold me, help me!	... Držte mne, braňte mne!

GRANDMOTHER BURYJA

What is this,	Ale dcero moje!
my daughter?	Ale dcero moje!

Hold me, help me!   Držte mne, braňte mne!

GRANDMOTHER BURYJA

Daughter,   Dcero, zase
you are ill again.   blouzniš, blouzniš!

Števa runs off, but in the doorway bumps into Karolka, who seizes him by the hand.

KOSTELNIČKA

They've all come for me.   To jdou pro mne, pro mne!

Scene Nine.

KAROLKA

Števa, this is terrible . . .   Števo, to je ti strašné . . .
Now the wedding's ruined . . .   Svatba pokažena . . .
Oh, if I were the bride,   Já být nevěstou,
how I'd weep.   plakala bych.

JENŮFA
(outside)

O God! O God!   Ó Bože, můj Bože,
That is my baby, my baby!   to je můj chlapčok, můj chlapčok!

ŠTEVA

All that noise out there makes me tremble, Jak by mi ten křik nohy podt'al,
and now I feel afraid.   a úzko je mi včil.

Jenůfa tries to free herself from Laca's grasp, but he drags her inside.

LACA

Jenůfa! Jenůfa!   Jenůfa, Jenůfa!
Try to pull yourself together!   Vzpamatuj se,
What dreadful things you are saying!   Co tě to hrozného napadlo!
People are listening!   Lidé to slyší!
Oh, try to pull yourself together!   Ó vzpamatuj se!

JENŮFA

Let me go!   Pust' mne,
That is Števuska, my baby.   to je Števuška, můj chlapčok,
Mine, mine!   můj, můj!

The Mayor enters, in his hand, baby clothes and a little red cap. Behind him, the other people.

Scene Ten.

JENŮFA

Ha, there now, you see his baby clothes!   Ha, vidite, jeho poviják,
There's his cap too!   jeho čepčáček!
I myself have made it from my own ribbons. Sama jsem ho ze svych pantli popravila!

MAYOR'S WIFE

Did you hear that?   Slyšiš rychtáři!
They know all about it!   Oni o tom vědi!

JENŮFA

You people,   Ej lidé,
what a way to bury him,   kterak jste ho dopravili?
neither coffin nor a wreath!   Bez truhélky, bez věnečku!

VILLAGE WOMAN

Jesus Maria!   Ježiši Kriste!
Can she herself have killed the baby?   Tak utratila svoje dítě!

Now you won't even let him rest!	Co mu pokoja nedáte?
Why must you drag him out in the ice and snow.	Kdesi ve sněhu a ledu s nim gúlali!
Števa, Števa!	Števo, mlynáři,
Quick you must run after them!	Běž za nima, honem běž,
It is your baby!	to je tvoje dítě!

THE MAYOR

Well, I think I've found the answer by myself.	To už jsem snad bar bez pánů na stopě!
There is no one higher than me here,	Já musim býtprvni ouřad...

(wiping the sweat from his brow)

yet, I wish that I were somewhere else!	... a, a raděj bych se neviděl!

CHORUS

Death to the murderess! *etc.*	Kamenim po ni!

LACA

Just let one of you lay a hand upon her!	Jenom se odvažte někdo se ji dotkout!
With his life he'll pay for it!	Život vás to bude stát!
Ah! I will kill you all!	Pěsti vás dobiju!

KOSTELNIČKA
(pulling herself together with an effort)

Now listen to me!	Ještě jsem tu já!
You know nothing about it!	Vy ničeho nevíte!
That deed was mine, mine the punishment!	To můj skutek můj trest boži!

CHORUS

Kostelnička!	Kostelnička!

KOSTELNIČKA

Yes, it was I who killed Jenůfa's baby!	Já jsem dítě Jenůfčino uničila...
I, I alone!	já samotná.
I was thinking of her future,	Její život,
her future happiness.	jeji štěsti
I felt ashamed and guilty that my foster-daughter's life should come to ruin!	Tiskla se na mne hanba, že jsem pastorkyni do zkázy dochovala!

(sinking to her knees)

O God in heaven, You should know that it was too much to bear;	Tys, Bože, to věděl, že to nebylo k sneseni,
that if the child had stayed alive,	že by se misto dítěte
two lives would have been utterly ruined completely.	utratily životy dva...
Jenůfa never went to Vienna;	Jenůfa nebyla ve Vidni,
I kept her hidden here.	já jsem ji schovávala,
I took the child,	omámila,
after I'd drugged her,	dítě vzala,
down to the river,	k řece zanesla,
and where the ice was cut,	a v prosekaný
I pushed it in!	otvor vstrčila.

CHORUS

Jesus Maria!	Ježiši Kriste,
Our own Kostenlička! *etc.*	to že Kostelnička!

KOSTELNIČKA

It was at night,	Bylo to večer.
not a sound came from the baby...	Ono se nebránilo...
not the slightest struggle...	ani nezapíplo...
I felt as though my hands had been set on fire,	Jen jako by mne na rukou pálilo...

and since that moment, I have known that I'm a murderess. Afterwards I told Jenůfa that it died without regaining consciousness!	a od té chvíle cítila jsem, že jsem vražednice. Jenůfě jsem potom řekla, že její dítě v bezvědomí umřelo!

O mother, under the ice . . .	Ej mamičko, pod led . . .

KOSTELNIČKA

Have mercy on my daughter. Do not blame her . . .	Och slitujte se nad ní, nechaňte ji . . .

JENŮFA
(*with fury*)

Away from me!	och! Nechte mne!

KOSTELNIČKA

. . . she is quite innocent . . . for I, I'm the one who's guilty!	Ona je nevinná . . . Mne suďte, mne kamenujte, bídnou!

KAROLKA
(*to Števa, who, quite shattered, leans against the window*)

Števa, is all this on your conscience?	Števo, to ty máš na svědomí?

(*flinging her arms around her mother's neck*)

Mamička, I feel so faint, I can hardly breathe! Take me out of here!	Mamičko, mně je tak těžko k zamdlení. Vyveďte mne ven,

THE MAYOR'S WIFE

Karolka, darling!	Karolka moja!

LACA

God in heaven, God in heaven! I have been the cause of this; I cut your cheek and disfigured you, that was why Števa left you, from that moment everything turned into misfortune!	Och, Bože můj, Bože můj, já jsem toho příčina, já ti to líco zohavil, aby te Števa nechal, a tak potom všechno došlo na to neštěstí!

KAROLKA

I will never marry Števa. I would rather jump in the river! Take me home! Take me home!	Já za Števa nepůjdu . . . raději bych to vody skočila, Pojďme dom! Pojďme dom!

MAID

He'll never find a girl who will marry him. That is his punishment —	To je na něho trest. Žádná děvčica za něho nepůjde —

Karolka rushes out, followed by her mother.

he won't even get a gipsy girl to take him!	co by jen poctivá cikánka byla!

Števa covers his face with his hands and hurries out. Grandmother Buryja, completely shattered, is led out by the maid.

Scene Eleven.

JENŮFA
(*to Kostelnička*)

Do not kneel, dear mother! There's been enough humiliation and torture already!	Vstaňte, pěstounko moja! Dosti smrtelného ponížení a muk vás čeka!

She raises Kostelnička up.

75

KOSTELNIČKA

Why, oh why do you raise me up?	Kam mne pozdvihuješ?
	(*with horror*)
See, they will take me away!	už to chápu, už to chápu,
	(*shrieks*)
Ah!	Óch!

She rushes towards the bedroom with the intention of killing herself.

No, no!	Ne, ne.
I must not!	Já nesmím!
If I did they would turn on you,	Oni by tebe soudili,
Jenůfa!	Jenůfo!

JENUFA

Ah mother, now I understand	A ta moje pěstounka,
at last! Ah no!	už to chápu,
No! We mustn't curse her.	není proklínaní hodna.
Do not condemn her,	Nezatracujte ji!
give her time to make atonement!	Dopřejte ji času k pokání!
The Saviour will look down on her!	Aji na ni Spasitel pohlédne!

LACA

Jenůfa,	Jenůfka,
surely you have lost your senses!	neusel ti rozum s cesty?

KOSTELNIČKA

If only you'll forgive me,	Odpusť mi jenom ty,
now I see I've thought more of myself than	včil už vidím, že jsem sebe milovala
I have thought of you, child,	víc než tebe,
you can say no longer:	Včil už nemůžeš volat:
'Mamička, ah mamička.'	'Mamičko, aj mamičko!'
You could not inherit my character or my blood,	tys nemohla dědit moji povahu, moji krev,
yet now, I come to you for strength . . .	a já z tebe včil beru sílu . . .
to suffer, for the Saviour will look down on me!	Chci trpět, trpět! Aji na mne Spasitel pohlédne!

JENUFA

God give you comfort!	Pánbůh vás potěš!

KOSTELNIČKA

Come, Mayor, lead me away!	Pojď te, rychtáň, veď te mne!

JENUFA

God give you comfort!	Pánbůh vás potěš!

The Mayor supports Kostelnička and leads her away, the rest of the people pushing out after them. Jenůfa and Laca remain.

Scene Twelve.

JENUFA

They have gone!	Odešli.
Now you go!	Jdi také!
Surely you see now	Však včil vidíš,
that my miserable life cannot ever be linked with yours.	že s mým bédným životem svůj spojit nemůžeš!
So go now!	Buď s Bohem . . .
But remember this; that you were always, always for me the best and finest man of all!	a pamatuj si, žes byl nejlepší člověk, nejlepší člověk.
Though you meant to hurt me when you cut my cheek, I forgave you long ago.	Žes mi zúmyslně poranil to líco, to jsem ti dávno odpustila.
You sinned only out of love,	To jsi hřešil jenom z lásky,
just as I did — once.	jako já — kdysi.

76

So, now you are going forth,
seeking a better life and you won't take me
   with you, Jenufa?

Ty odejdeš do svĕta
za hodnĕjšin životem a mne nevezmeš s
   sebou,
Jenůfka?

JENUFA

You know they'll call me to the trial,
just think how contemptuously everyone
   will look at me!

Viš, že mne budou volat k soudu,
že každý se na mne s opovržením podiva?

LACA

Jenůfka,
I would bear far more than that for you!
What does the world matter,
if only we are together!

Jenůfka,
já i to pro tebe snesu!
Co nám do svĕta,
když si budeme na utĕchu?

JENUFA

O Laca,
Dearest Laca!
Oh, come! Oh, come!
The love that I feel in my heart for you tells
   me
that God
at last has smiled on us!

O Laco,
duša moja!
O pojd', o pojd'!
Včil k tobĕ mne dovedla láska ta vĕtši,

co Pánbůh
s ni spokojen!

Curtain.

*Sylvia Fisher as Kostelnička in the first production of 'Jenůfa' at Covent Garden, in 1956
(photo: Houston Rogers, Theatre Museum)*

A Russian Heart of Darkness

Alex de Jonge

Alexander Nikolaevich Ostrovsky (1823-1886) was two years younger than Dostoevsky, and shared his interest in the darker side of the Russian psyche. The son of a civil servant who worked in the law courts, he followed in his father's footsteps to work in the offices of the Moscow commercial courts. The fifty plays he left behind him at his death lie at the centre of the Russian repertoire of realistic theatre.

There is precious little delicacy about Ostrovsky's work. Technically speaking his plays are crude; the characterisation is blocked out in primary colours and plot design dispenses with anything approaching finesse. A historian of world theatre would doubtless discover that the plays read like clumsy imitations of Musset's *Comedies et Proverbes*, or worse, like bad Diderot, which is as bad as any play can get. Yet it would be a great mistake to dismiss Ostrovsky's work because of its spectacular lack of technical virtuosity.

His experience in the courts of Moscow introduced him to the remarkable world of the Russian merchant, a world which as a writer Ostrovsky made his own, and which the critic Dobrolyubov christened 'The Dark Kingdom'. Merchants were less a class than an hereditary caste in 19th-century Russia, immediately distinguishable from the gentry by their dress, their speech, their habits, their names even. They ranged from petty traders who cheated and grafted their way through life surviving on tiny margins of profit, to some of the greatest and wealthiest families in the land. It was said that there were enough furs to be found in the merchant warehouses of Moscow to lay a path from the Kremlin to the Louvre. The merchant world was regulated according to the dominant principles of cunning and dishonesty, a world in which everyone owed it to himself to cheat his neighbour and all other comers as often and as successfully as possible. It also constituted the inward looking and secretive conservative heartland of Russian culture, a world which the westernising reforms of Peter the Great and Catherine had passed by and ignored. Merchants still lived according to the sombre codes of Old Muscovy, as spelt out in the 16th-century handbook of etiquette *Domostroi, The Household Builder*, which encouraged a man to be master of his house and made its position on the role of women crystal clear by encouraging a husband to keep his wife in order by beating her frequently and tenderly. Merchants also tended to be conservative on matters of religion; repudiating the ecclesiastical reforms of the 17th century, they tended towards conservative heresy and sectarianism. The merchant world projected an image of patriarchal authoritarianism, and cruel domestic oppression taking place within dark and private mansions in which young wives pined away or 'dried up', sons were bullied mercilessly by their fathers and luckless servants beaten to death. Yet at the same time this was also a world of greed and great appetites, in which the instincts were repressed but never eliminated, and in which passions could burst forth in acts of wild and extravagant rebellion.

In *The Idiot* Dostoevsky gives us a superb evocation of the dark kingdom, which has the sexual obsessive and eventual murderer Parfyen Rogozhin as its chief inhabitant.

Ostrovsky's evocations of merchant life which range from the dramatic to the comic are fascinating in themselves. For example, most of his plays feature numerous loony pilgrims, opportunist holy fools and hysterical wise women who wander eccentrically on and off stage, and are fed and housed by devout and usually gullible merchants' wives, giving us a unique insight into the kind of world in which the Holy Man Rasputin made his debut. Moreover the plays provide the speaker of Russian with a treasury of gloriously fat idioms, turns of phrase and juicy linguistic idiosyncrasies. In other words, they have a lot to offer anyone who enjoys wallowing in a certain form of Russian ethnicity, which has musical equivalents to be heard in the work of virtually every Russian composer from Glinka to Stravinsky, and whose charm, for some, appears to be inexhaustible.

But there is far more to Ostrovsky's world than a theatrical rendering of a Slavic version of the Blues, and more in play here than the colourful evocation of a long vanished world. Just as Balzac's peasant misers and financial calculators provide an invaluable insight into *mentalités* that are as prevalent in contemporary France as they ever were in the days of the July Monarchy, so Ostrovsky's evocations of the dark kingdom have a relevance that endures beyond the world of Muscovite merchants.

Writing some thirty years after Ostrovsky, Leon Trotsky recognised that it would require something far more radical than a political upheaval to change Russia; first and foremost the culture had to be purged of certain fundamental patterns of social, and ultimately spiritual and also intellectual, thuggery and vileness which, for him, were symbolised by: 'Two streams of Russian abuse — the swearing of masters, officials and police, full and fat, and the hungry, desperate and tormented swearing of the masses, that have coloured the whole of Russian life with their despicable patterns.'

Ostrovsky's plays provide a magnificent account of certain streams of Russian abuse, and Russian oppression, which have a relevance far beyond their immediate milieu. For example, the oppressive authoritarianism with which the older generation keeps youth in check is merely a particular manifestation of a game that has long been and will long remain the Russian national sport: that passion for telling others how they should conduct their lives, which comes to a peak in that delighted glee with which a Russian will inform you that you are doing wrong, whether you are illegally photographing a strategic object such as a 19th-century bridge across the Moskva River or, horror of horrors, allowing your child out on a winter's day attired in what the local grandmothers decide is an insufficiency of clothes. Ostrovsky's merchants may have perished with the revolution, but if you look hard enough you will find that his dark kingdom is still very much with us.

Curiously Ostrovsky's most famous play, *The Storm* (1860), is set not in Moscow but in a stifling provincial town upon the Volga. Characteristically unsubtle in plot and characterisation, it remains a wonderfully powerful evocation of the savage bullying repression of the young by the old. The censor who wanted the playwright to cut Katya Kabanova's mother out of the play altogether, because he considered her to be a veiled portrait of Tsar Nicholas I can only be considered an inspired lunatic, for she is the embodiment of petty, silly and sadistic authority. However as far as we know Nicholas never employed the kind of barbarous emotional blackmail which Kabanova *mère* applies to her unfortunate son Tichon. Tichon is too much an archetype to be given an individual character. In many respects he is Great Russian man and husband; fundamentally kind and gentle but desperately weak in the face of strong female authority, his only recourse is withdrawal into the benign world of drink. Tichon's equivalent is to be seen any evening on the Moscow metro, smiling weakly in his drunkenness as he reclines against the shoulder of a strong and silent woman who stares steadfastly into the middle distance catching no-one's eye, and who is waiting for tomorrow's remorseful hangover to give her man hell.

The play evokes the intolerable violence of domestic relations in the dark kingdom, which might indeed be considered a political metaphor for Russia both past and present insofar as it is a place in which no-one has any kind of redress against or escape from authority, and in which one is either a master or a victim, a world of ordinary misery and ordinary despair.

It is also a superb study in sexual frustration and violent sexual release. Ostrovsky is not particularly good at character or motive. Considered in terms of the well-made play Katya Kabanova is a peculiarly summary creation: for example her readiness to sleep with her lover as soon as she gets the chance does not accord with her readiness to commit suicide out of sheer misery, shame and despair. Yet Ostrovsky is not trying for the well-made psychological play but reaching for something more basic. Thanks to the perfunctory characterisation, Katya is less an individual than a force of nature. Images such as the river, the storm, the flames of hell give the action an elemental feel of raw sexual energy, archetypal frustration and, eventually, absolute despair. The play becomes a remarkably moving study of an illicit passion, which admits of no resolution except for departure and death. It may lack the sophisticated poetry and psychological delicacies of *Tristan* or *Bérénice*, but it shares their unmistakable and despairing emotional tonalities, while creating a vision of life in a sleepy river-side town that takes us on a strange and disturbing journey into a peculiarly Russian Heart of Darkness.

'Jenůfa' in Cologne, 1981; Anny Schlemm as Grandmother Buryja and Josephine
Barstow in the title role (photo: Paul Leclaire)

William McAlpine as Boris and Amy Shuard as Katya Kabanova at Sadler's Wells in
1951 (photo: Angus McBean © Harvard Theatre Collection)

'Katya Kabanova' at Scottish Opera; (left to right) John Robertson as Tichon, Kerstin
Meyer as Kabanicha and William McCue as Dikoy (photo: Eric Thorburn)

Janáček's forgotten commentary on 'Katya Kabanova'

John Tyrrell

Dear Friend,
   Are you in Prague?
   Mr Julius Wolfsohn (Cologne, Habsburgerring 1) wrote to me from Cologne.
   He wants some facts from me for a preparatory article which he wishes to write, to say something before the première of *Katya Kabanova* in Cologne.
   I have no idea what I should write. I enclose his letter. Can you help?
   Although I will also write to him, I don't want to mix up my mental juices [literally: brain pulp]. In fact I can't, for I am already in a different atmosphere.[1]

By the date of writing, August 22, 1922, Janáček was most certainly in another mental world. In this letter to his friend the writer Max Brod, the translator of his operas and an active promoter of his works, he went on to say how he was writing out the libretto of *The Cunning Little Vixen* (roughly at the last act, he reported). He also asked Brod whether he knew Karel Čapek's *RUR* and *From the Life of the Insects*, adding 'his sister said something about a libretto' — the first hint of interest in *The Makropulos Case*.

Brod, in his reply of August 31, undertook to send Wolfsohn his 'essays about Katya'. This he seems not to have done for in his correspondence with Brod on October 11, 1922, Janáček mentioned that 'that man from Cologne' had written to him again, asking for Brod's contribution. The Cologne première of *Katya Kabanova*, the first foreign production of the opera (under Otto Klemperer), was now imminent. Brod replied that Janáček should send Wolfsohn his 'review of Katya', an extended piece only briefly devoted to the Brno première of 1921 — most of the rest eventually found its way into Brod's chapter on the opera in his biography of the composer.[2] Wolfsohn, however, wrote again. His letter to Janáček dated November 1 has survived in the Janáček Archive in Brno and in it he announced that the Cologne première was expected between November 20 and 25 (in fact it took place on December 8) and asked Janáček about the meaning of several motifs from the opera which he had written out on a separate sheet.

That Janáček really did write to Wolfsohn about *Katya Kabanova* and took the trouble to identify the motifs was, however, something that has remained unknown for the past sixty years. Julius Wolfsohn, a pianist (pupil of Leschetizky) and teacher, later turned journalist, fled Germany for the United States in 1933, taking with him two letters from Janáček, written in German. In 1944, at the age of 64, he died in New York. That same year the two letters were acquired, through a New York antiquarian dealer, by the distinguished Yugoslav-American musicologist Dragan Plamenac. Plamenac, however, made no attempt to make their contents known until 1981 when, shortly before his own death, he published a facsimile of both letters, accompanied by a brief commentary in Serbo-Croat.

1 *Korespondence Leoš Janáčeka s Maxem Brodem*, ed. A. Raktorys & J. Racek (Prague, 1953)
2 M. Brod: *Leoš Janáček: život a dílo* (Prague, 1924; Ger. orig., 1925, rev.2/1956)

We know something about the inspirational sources of *Katya Kabanova* from Janáček's correspondence with Kamila Stösslová,[3] but, unlike the cases of *Jenůfa*, *Brouček* or the *Vixen*, Janáček published no commentary on the opera apart from the brief references he made to it in his 1924 autobiography, or his feuilleton on the Berlin première. His letters to Wolfson about the opera, intended to help in the promotion of this work, are thus all the more precious in providing an unique semi-official view.

Esteemed Sir,
    I am pleased that *Katya Kabanova* will be performed in Cologne. But how exactly can I help you?
    The work flowed from my pen just like the beautiful river Volga. Should I now catch the waves? Impossible. The motifs transform themselves in my work as if 'on their own'.
    It seems to me that even when a motif rises up threateningly it has its seed in the still, dreaming waters. For instance the motif (ex. 1) threads its way through the whole work. The whole weight of the drama lies in it. But also the cause: the departure of Tichon. And the motif flies now into the flutes, the sleighbells and the oboes (ex. 2).

And when a motif becomes so different, I feel that it must be so. I don't think anything more about it.
    Also I don't think any more about *Katya Kabanova*. I am already taken up with another, different work.
    I have asked Dr Max Brod to stand by to help you.
    I am most obliged and grateful to you.
    I hope the performance is successful. But it is no easy thing!
        Respectfully yours,
                    Leoš Janáček
Ukvaly [Hukvaldy], 2.IX.1922

This letter emphasises, as does Janáček's reference to the work in his autobiography, the central symbolism of the Volga, as well as the importance of the opening motto theme. Equally well, however, the letter gives one of the clearest statements made by Janáček about how instinctive and non-intellectual the process of opera composing was for him. The work flowed effortlessly from his pen, and the way that the themes change was something that was not controlled by rational thought. If changes in them seemed right, he made them.
    In view of Janáček's refusal to 'catch the waves' it seems all the more odd that with his second letter Wolfsohn was able to coax Janáček to 'identify' themes from the opera, the only instance in any opera where Janáček provided such a direct interpretation. In his second letter, dated Brno November 2, 1922 and written immediately on receipt of Wolfsohn's, Janáček simply took

3 see J. Tyrrell. *Leoš Janáček: Kat'a Kabanová* (Cambridge, 1982), 92ff

Wolfsohn's piece of manuscript paper, with its seven themes neatly written out (with page and rehearsal numbers from the recently published vocal score), labelled them with letters and in some cases with short verbal tags (ex. 3), and on the other side of the sheet, provided rather lengthier explanations. In this translation, Wolfsohn's numbers and locations are given in italic, then Janáček annotations above the themes (mostly in quotation marks) followed by the comments Janáček made on the back of the sheet:

no. 1, p. 7 rehearsal number 5
  a 'lightning'; the motif (a) is from the storm (lightning)
no. 2, p. 8 rehearsal number 6
  b1 'reproach'; with motif b1 b2 *Katya* bears the reproaches of *Kabanicha*
no. 3, p. 16, rehearsal number 15, 1
  c2 from the Dikoy motif c [here Janáček added a short motif]; the motif
  c, c2 is from Dikoy's characterisation
no. 4, p. 16 rehearsal no. 15, bar 3
  b2 [no other comment by Janáček]
no. 5, p. 27, 3/8 bar, quaver = 56
  d1 'Katya's unstained purity'; motif d, d2 is from Katya's characterisation
no. 6, p. 71, introductory bars
  e [bar 1] 'Suffocating atmosphere', 'air filled with evil', d2 [bars 2-3];
  motif e is the suffocating gloom in the scene with the key
no. 7, p. 86, introduction
  f 'The heart misses a beat'; motif f, f1 Boris's heart misses a beat in the
  moment that Katya approaches

Seen in the light of the interpretations of Brod and his successors, none of Janáček's comments are particularly startling. Some in fact do little more than identify the place in the score, though it is useful to have Janáček's remarks on the atmosphere of the prelude to Act Two, scene one, (Wolfsohn's no. 6). It should be stressed that the selection of themes is Wolfsohn's, not Janáček's, though in one case — c — Janáček felt obliged to fill in a further theme. Perhaps the most interesting features of the exercise were the arrows that Janáček drew to connect the last five notes of Wolfsohn's second theme (Janáček's b1) with his fourth theme (Janáček's b2), and to connect Wolfsohn's fifth and sixth themes (Janáček's d1 and d2), revealing that however unconscious were the origins of the thematic transformations, Janáček became aware of them. His letter concludes with the following comment:

> I am convinced that from the motifs abcdef not only a1 a2 b1 b2 c1 c2 d1 d2 *etc.* each according to the situation, but also a1 a2 a3 a4 b1 b2 b3 *etc.* are to be found in the work.

> The motifs must not *fade*, they must *live* continuously, they must *hold themselves in life.*

> With thanks for your letter. Yours respectfully
> Leoš Janáček

Note: D. Plamenac's article appeared as 'Nepoznati komentari Leoša Janáčeka operi "Katja Kabanova"', *Muzikološki zbornik*, xvii (1981), 122-30

The English National Opera 1973 production of 'Katya Kabanova' by John Blatchley, designed by Stefanos Lazaridis with (left to right) Moira Clark as Feklusha, Robert Ferguson as Tichon, Elizabeth Connell as Kabanicha, Barbara Walker as Varvara, Sheila Rex as Glasha and Ava June in the title role (photo: Donald Southern)

Katya Kabanova

An Opera in Three Acts by Leoš Janáček
based on Ostrovsky's *The Storm*

English translation by Norman Tucker

Katya Kabanova was first performed in Brno on October 23, 1921.
The first performance in England was at Sadler's Wells Theatre on
April 10, 1951. The first performance in the United States was at
Karamu House, Cleveland on November 26, 1957 with piano, then at
the Empire State Music Festival, Bear Mountain on August 2, 1960.

The set for Act Two of 'Katya Kabanova' in Brno

CHARACTERS

Vanya Kudryash (Váňa Kudrjáš) *Dikoy's clerk*	*tenor*
Glasha (Glaša) *a servant*	*mezzo-soprano*
Dikoy (Dikoj) *a rich merchant*	*bass*
Boris Grigoryevich (Grigorjevič) *his nephew*	*tenor*
Feklusha (Fekluša) *a servant*	*mezzo-soprano*
Marfa Ignatevna Kabanova known as Kabanicha	
a rich merchant's widow	*contralto*
Tichon *her son*	*tenor*
Varvara *foster-child in the Kabanov household*	*mezzo-soprano*
Katerina Kabanova, known as Katya	
(Káťa Kabanová) *Tichon's wife*	*soprano*
Kuligin *a friend of Vanya*	*baritone*

Time: about 1860
Place: the little town of Kalinov on the banks of the Volga

Note: Norman Tucker spelt the characters' names following the convention of
Russian transliteration rather than Czech.

Act One

A park above the steep Volga bank with a distant view of the countryside. To the right the Kabanovs' house. Seats beside the path, shrubbery. Afternoon sun.

VANYA KUDRYASH
(seated, gazing at the river)

Wonderful! Really one must say so, it's wonderful.	Zázrak! Vskutku třeba řci, že zázrak.

Glasha emerges from the Kabanovs' house.

Glasha! Just think of it, day after day I sit here and gaze on this river, and still I never weary of it.	Glašo! Vidiš, brachu, dvacet pět let už denně se dívám na Volhu a nemohu se vynadívat.

GLASHA

What of that?	Nu, a co?

KUDRYASH

Loveliest of rivers! Its beauty fills one with happiness.	Neobyčejný pohled! Ta krása! Duše se raduje.

GLASHA

Oh, what nonsense!	To je toho!

KUDRYASH

Glorious! And you say: "Oh, what nonsense!" Take a good look at it, see what beauty's hidden in nature.	Rozkoš! A ty jen "To je toho!" Měla bys jen přihlédnout, jaká krása tají se v přírodě!

GLASHA

Well of course! You are always right. You're the clever one, chemist, a scientist.	Nu, arci! Jaká s tebou řeč! Jsi učitel, chemik, mechanik!

KUDRYASH

Look, Glasha! Who's that fellow waving his arms about?	Podivej se, kdo to tam tak rozkládá rukama!

GLASHA

That's Dikoy, bullying his nephew again.	To Dikoj, vadí se se synovcem.

KUDRYASH

Here where it's so peaceful!	To si našel místo!

GLASHA

You know what he's like. Always finding fault with poor Boris Grigoryevich.	Najde si je všude. Upadl mu do rukou Boris Grigorjevič.

KUDRYASH

What a savage brute he is! Always got his teeth into someone.	Tak si na něm pojezdi! Jakoby se od řetězu utrh'!

Dikoy and Boris approach. Glasha runs off to the house; Kudryash saunters off across the park.

Don't let him see us; or perhaps he'll turn on us too!	Pojďme mu s cesty! Ještě by se na nás chytil!

DIKOY
(to Boris)

Lazy rascal! Why d'you keep on hanging round me? Get off back home with you!	Darmochlebe! Přišel jsi sem lelky chytat? Ať se mi ztratíš!

BORIS	
What would I do at home on Sunday?	Co budu doma dělat? Je svátek.
DIKOY	
You would find something if you tried!	Najdeš si práci, jenom chtít!
You have heard me say,	Řekl jsem ti už,
not once, not twice, thirty times:	jednou, dvakrát, třikrát:
"Stay right away from me, right away from me!"	"Nechoď mi na oči! Nechoď mi na oči!"
But you never listen. Can't you leave me alone?	Ale všecko marno. Máš snad málo místa?
If I turn round you're at my elbow!	Kam se zvrtnu, všude tě potkám.
Pah! Lazy dog! Don't just stand there!	Fuj, proklatče! Co tu stojíš?
Can you hear me or not?	Mluvím k tobě, či ne?
BORIS	
I'm listening! What d'you want then?	Vždyť slyším! Co mám dělat?
DIKOY	
You can just go to hell.	Aby ses propadl!
(to Glasha, standing at the Kabanovs' doorway)	
Look at him lounging about all day long!	Vida ho, jak se na člověka věší!
Is your mistress at home?	Je baryňa doma?
GLASHA	
She's at church still.	Je v sadu.
Dikoy spits and walks off.	
KUDRYASH	
(taking a step towards Boris)	
You and your uncle never agreed.	Copak s ním máte za jednání?
None of us can understand	Nemůžu toho pochopit, že se vám chce
why you should choose to live with him	žít u něho a snášet nadávky.
and be bullied and slave-driven.	
BORIS	
Not because I choose to — I must.	Kdež by se mi chtělo! Musím!
KUDRYASH	
Yes, but why must you, if I may ask?	Ale proč pak musíte, že se tak ptám?
BORIS	
There's no secret about it.	Proč bych neodpověděl?
D'you remember my grandmother?	Znal jste moji babičku?
KUDRYASH	
Anfisa Michailovna?	Anfisu Michajlovnu?
BORIS	
Father married well above his station.	Ta neměla tatínka ráda,
That offended my grandmother	proto, že si vzal šlechtičnu.
and that's why my parents lived in	Z té příčiny žili v Moskvě.
Moscow. Mother used to say to me:	Maminka říkávala
on no account would she ever live with those provincials!	že nemohla ani tři dny s rodinou se snésti.
KUDRYASH	
Who could blame her!	Darmo mluvit!
BORIS	
Couldn't get used to the thought of it.	Vše jí připadalo tak kruté!

Other folk's ways of living are not our ways.	To by si člověk musil příliš zvykat.

BORIS

Our parents were not rich but they spent all they had on us,	Rodiče nás v Moskvě dobře vychovali,
stinting themselves so that we should not suffer.	ničeho pro nás nelitovali.
I was sent to the Academy of Commerce.	Mne dali do obchodní akademie
My sister went away to boarding school.	a sestru do pensionátu.
Then quite suddenly they both fell ill and died of cholera.	Ale potom oba zemřeli na choleru
We two were left alone in the world, I and my sister.	a já se sestrou jsme zůstali sirotami.
And then I heard that my grandmother too had died here,	Proto slyším, že také babička tady zemřela
and left us both some money; Uncle was to let us have it	a zanechala závět, aby nás strýc vyplatil,
when we were twenty-one — on one condition . . .	až budem plnoleti. S podmínkou —

KUDRYASH

What was that?	Jakou?

BORIS

That we did what Uncle Dikoy said.	— budeme-li k němu uctivi.

KUDRYASH

Oh, then I'm afraid you won't see much of your legacy.	Tak, to vaše záležitost špatně dopadá!

BORIS

If I were alone I would have left him long ago,	Kdybych já byl sám, nechal bych vše a ujel bych.
but I'm sorry for my sister. He wants her here.	Ale sestry je mi líto. Už pro ni psal,
But till now my mother's family have stopped her coming.	ale maminčini příbuzní ji nepustili.
What a life for a girl like my sister!	Jaký byl by to pro ni zde život?
Think of her in this place. It's terrible.	To pomyšlení je mi strašlivé.

KUDRYASH

What a life. What a petty tyrant!	O jé! Jaký neurvalec!

Glasha goes up to Feklusha as she enters.

What is it?	Co pak je?
Oh, it must be the people coming back from evening service.	Snad už nechodí lidé z večerní bohoslužby?
God be with you. I must go.	Nuž s Bohem, půjdu též.

BORIS

No, stay here. Stay for a moment.	Posečkej! Posečkej ještě!
How my youth is passing! How quickly it is passing.	Hubim svoje mládí. Ó hubim svoje mládí!
Year in, year out, no happiness, no happiness.	Jará léta, jen strádání, jen strádání!
Has life no joy at all?	A radost života?
Grasp it and suddenly it vanishes!	Hledej ji v blednoucich červáncich!

FEKLUSHA
(to Glasha)

Lovely, isn't it. Yes, dearie! Lovely! Wonderful!	Krása je to, má milá! Krása, spanilost!
That's all I can say! That's all I can say!	Nač o tom mluvit? Nač o tom mluvit?

All of them so good and pious, most of all Kabanicha!

Jaci lide bohabojni, štědři, ti Kabanovych!

BORIS

Kabanicha!

Kabanovych?!

Feklusha goes off into the house with Glasha.

KUDRYASH

She's a hypocrite. Full of alms and charities.
But inside that house she wields a rod of iron.

Je to svatoušek, žebráky poděluje,
ale domaci by k smrti ukousala.

BORIS

Am I awake or dreaming? Oh, what folly! Why must I fall in love?

Chodim jak omameny. Nač, to ještě? Zamilovat se ještě!

KUDRYASH

It's love, is it?

A do koho?

BORIS

She's married.
Look. There she is coming, his mother's with her.
Oh, I must be crazy, I must be crazy!

Do vdane!
Hle, tady jde s mužem a tchyně s nimi.
Nuž, nejsem-li hlupak? Nejsem-li hlupak?

KUDRYASH

You had better forget her,
Katya is not like other girls.

Toho musite nechat,
nechcete-li ji zahubit.

BORIS

Come here, let's take just one look at her.

Podivejme se na ni za rohem!

Boris and Kudryash step back to the side of the house. Enter from the other direction Katya, Varvara, Kabanicha and Tichon.

And then run back home. Ha, ha!

A potom běž domů. Cha! Cha! Cha! Cha!

He and Vanya disappear behind the house.

KABANICHA
(*to Tichon*)

If you want to obey your mother,
then you will go as your father used to,
to Kazan, to the market there, and today.

Chceš-li matky poslechnout,
pojedeš na trh do Kazaně,
kam otec vždy jezdival. A to dnes!

TICHON

Of course I'll do as you ask.

Nu, jak vas neposlechnout!

KABANICHA

I would believe you,
but I see just the opposite every day,
see it and hear it, every day here.
You can't deny it, you put your wife above your own mother.
It's very plain you do not care for me
as you did once before you were married.

Věřila bych ti,
kdybych vlastnima očima neviděla,
na vlastni uši neslyšela;
už davno vidim, že je ti žena matky milejši!
Už od těch dob, co jsi se oženil,
nepozoruji dřivějši lasky.

TICHON

When do you notice it?

V čempak to shledavate?

KABANICHA

All the time. In my heart I know at once when you keep things from me.

Ve všem! Co nevidim očima, o tom povi srdce!

TICHON

Oh, but Mama dear, that's no way to talk.

Ale maminko! Co vas napada!

I respect and honour you just like my own mother.	Pro mne jste vy, maminko, jako rodná matka.
These are foolish thoughts. And Tichon loves you just as I do.	Co vás napadá? A Tichon má vás také rád.

KABANICHA

You should keep your mouth shut.	Ty bys mohla mlčet, mohla mlčet!
Nobody has asked you. Why should you defend him?	Nikdo se tě neptal. Nezastávej se ho.
Nothing will happen to him.	Vždyť ti ho neubude,
He, after all, is my son.	Vždyť je to také můj syn.

VARVARA

Oh, what a place to choose for a sermon!	Našla si místo pro svoje kázání.

KABANICHA

Interfering like that! Making yourself conspicuous,	Co jsi vyskočila? Do očí sebou zavrtět.
so that all may see how much you love your husband!	Aby viděli snad, jak máš muže ráda?

KATYA

Words like these were best unspoken. Why should you insult me?	To mi říkat nemusíte. Proč mne urážíte?
I have never harmed you.	Trpět pro nic za nic.
In front of others or by myself I am the same still.	Ať před lidmi či bez lidí, vždycky jsem stejná.

Exit into the house.

KABANICHA

See how proud the girl is! Why should I insult her?	Vida, vážný ptáček. Hned se urazila.

(to Tichon)

Once perhaps you loved me, before you were married. Ah, but now you've a wife ...	Možná, žes měl matku rád, dokuds byl sám, ale teď, co máš ženu ...

TICHON

My wife is one person, you are another. I love you both.	Jedno druhému nepřekáží; obě mám rád.

KABANICHA

Do you put your wife before your own mother?	Tak tedy ženu za matku měníš?
A wife should know her place!	A pak se tě má bát,
If you're soft with her how can she ever respect you?	když po tvojím se ženou všeho jen s láskou?
You'd give in to her? What if she takes a lover?	Ani pohrozit? Ať si má třeba milence?

TICHON

Oh, but Mama, Katya loves me.	Ale maminko, vždyť mne má ráda!

KABANICHA

Would that be so small a thing? Would you say nothing?	To snad také nic není? Ani okřiknout?

TICHON

Oh, but dear Mama!	Ale maminko!

KABANICHA

Yes, you'd just stand and say nothing.	No mluv to také nic není?

TICHON

This is really too much!	Ale na mou duši!

Stupid fool! You watch her. I'm going in.   Hlupáku! Jen pro hřích! Jdu domů.

Exit into the house.

TICHON
(to Varvara)

You see now! Always on at her!   Tak vidíš, pořád jen pro ni!

VARVARA

Well, is that your wife's fault?   Copak za to může?
Mother is always nagging her, so are you   Matka ji pronásleduje, a ty také!
too.
Then you come and tell me how much you   A pak ještě říkáš, že ji máš rád.
love her.
Why stand there doing nothing?   Co stojíš, přešlapuješ?
I can see quite clearly what's in your mind,   Na očích ti vidím, co by si rád:
Drunkard!   Zpit se!

Tichon lounges off in silence.

She is unhappy. She is so unhappy.   Je mi ji líto. Toť se ví, že líto.

She hesitates at the door.

How I love her!   Mám ji ráda.
Oh, how could anyone not love her?   Proč bych ji neměla mít ráda?

Scene Two. *A room in the Kabanovs' house.*

KATYA
(laying her embroidery aside)

I'm always wondering —   Víš, co mi napadlo?

VARVARA

What?   Co?

KATYA

Why can't we fly like birds?   Proč lidé nelétají?

VARVARA

I don't know what you mean!   Nechápu, co pravíš!

KATYA

Tell me this, why can't we fly away,   Povídám, proč lidé nelétají
just spread our wings and fly away?   Tak jako ptáci nelétají?
You know, sometimes I imagine   Víš, zdává se mi někdy, že jsem pták.
I can fly and spread my wings. Shall I show   Tak tě to láká vzlétnout! Chci to zkusit!
you?

She makes flying gestures.

VARVARA

What are you doing?   Co vyvádíš?

KATYA

I used to be so gay and happy,   Jaká jsem bývala rozpustilá!
but since I came here to live I have changed.   A u vás jsem docela uvadla.

VARVARA

Katya, d'you think I did not know?   Myslíš, že toho nevidím?

KATYA

Ah, then it was all so different.   Ach, byla jsem zcela jinší!
I had no longings for other things.   Žila jsem, po ničem netoužíc,
Freely as a bird I wandered!   jako ptáče na svobodě!
Mother knew nothing of my thoughts and   Maminka duše ve mně netušila,
longings.
I was treated like a baby.   strojila mne jak panenku!
D'you know how I spent my days at home?   Víš, jak jsem žila za svobodna?

Well, I will tell you.
I would rise quite early and if it were
  summer,
run to the spring nearby, and bathe in it.
Then I would bring water
and water all the flowers, every single one
  of them.

Hned ti to povím.
Vstávala jsem časně. Bylo-li to v létě
vyšla jsem ke studánce a umyla se.
Pak přinesu si vodičky
a všechny, všechny květinky v domě zaleju.

VARVARA

Just as you do here, Katya.

U nás je to zrovna tak!

KATYA

Then I would go to church.
I always loved so dearly to go to church.
I felt as if I were entering paradise.
Then I would see no-one, hear no-one, and

I never knew when the service each day
  was ended.
Afterwards Mama told me
people all round had looked at me,
seeing me act so strangely.
And then on a fine summer day
when columns of golden light fell aslant
  from the dome
and the incense in clouds went floating up,
I used to imagine I could see angels flying
aloft in the golden haze
of Heaven.
I would fall down on my knees and cry —
but I never knew what used to make me
  cry so.
So they would find me.
And all the visions I used to see, what
  visions!
Lofty golden cathedrals, high in the
  heavens,
and mountains and forests.
I felt as if I were flying, soaring and flying.
And all about me the sound of choirs
  invisible.

Po tom jsem šla do kostela.
Já k smrti ráda chodila do kostela.
Bývalo mi, jak bych stoupala do ráje.
Nikoho nevidím, neslyším, času
  nevnímám,
ani když bohoslužby končí.

Maminka říkávala,
že na mne všichni hleděli,
co se to se mnou děje!
A viš, za slunečního dne,
když s kopule padal takový světelný proud,

a v něm valil se dým jako oblaka,
a stávalo se mi, že jsem v tom sloupu
vidala litat anděly
a zpívat.
A já padnu na kolena a pláču;
a já sama nevím, proč modlím se a pláču.

Tak mě tam našli,
a jaké sny se mi zdávaly, jaké sny!

Jak bych viděla zlaté, vysoké chrámy

a hory a stromy,
a bylo mi, jak bych létala, vysoko létala,
a všude zpívají hlasy neviditelné!

VARVARA

Katya, oh, what is this?

Káťo, co je s tebou?

KATYA

The scent of the cypress.

A cypryše voní!

VARVARA

Oh, what is this?

Co je s tebou?

KATYA

A dreadful sin, dreadful sin,
as if the earth yawned in front of me and I
  was slipping, falling,
pushed by unseen hands to destruction.

Nějaký hřích na mne jde!
Jako bych stála nad propastí —
někdo mne do ní strkal
a já nemám za co se chytit.

VARVARA

Are you crazy?

Co se s tebou děje? Jsi zdráva?

KATYA

Crazy? Oh, how I wish I really knew! Deep
  in my inmost heart,
such strange desires are stirring!

Zdráva ... Raději bych byla nemocná.

Taková divná touha do hlavy mi leze

My will is powerless against them.
When I try to think my mind is confused
and bewildered.
When my tongue mutters a prayer,
all the time I am thinking something
very different.
Just as if the devil came to me then,
and whispered such horrible things.
It is too shameful even to think of it!
At night too.

a nikam nemohu ji uniknout.
Začnu přemýšlet, a nemohu myšlenky
sebrat.
Jazykem přemílám slova,
ale na mysli mi tane něco jiného.

Jakoby mi ďábel našeptával
a samé takové nedobré věci,
až je mi hanba před sebou samotnou.
A v noci —

VARVARA

What do you dream then?

Co se to zdává?

KATYA

Varya, I cannot sleep.
There is, all the time, someone near,
whispering to me.
Someone speaking so tenderly to me —
a voice soft as a dove,
someone embracing me so warmly,
calling me to go and live with him and I . . .
and I go, — I go with him.
Oh, but you, what can you know of it? A
child still!
Ah, but why tell you about all this? A child
still!

Varjo! Nemohu spat.
Pořad mně zní v uchu takové našeptávání;

kdosi se mnou tak laskavě mluví
jak když holub vrká,
jak by mne objimal tak vřele, tak vřele,
horoucně, jak by mne někam vedl, a —
a já jdu, a jdu — za nim!
Ale nač tobě to vykládam? Jsi divka!

Ale nač tobě to vykládam? Jsi divka!

VARVARA

Oh, tell me! I'm far worse than you!
Far worse than you! Tell me!

Ó, povidej! Jsem horši než ty!
Horši než ty! Povidej!

KATYA

I am too ashamed. Don't ask me.

Nuž, co povidat? Stydim se.

VARVARA

What need you be ashamed of? Who am I
to be your judge?
I have my sins too.

Neni třeba se stydět! Nač bych já tě
soudila?
Mam svoje hřichy.

KATYA

It is a terrible sin
to love another man.
What have I done? What will the end be?

Vždyť je to takovy hřich,
když miluji jineho.
Co si počnu? kam se poděju?

VARVARA

When your husband's gone perhaps you'll
see him?

Možna, že se uda s nim se vidět?

KATYA

No, no, no, no, no. No, never!
God forbid!

Ne, ne, ne, ne, ne, ne! Co mysliš?
Chraň Pan Buh!

VARVARA

And why?

Nu což?

Enter Tichon. Katya embraces him.

Surely she is mad.

Zblaznila jsi se?

She runs off.

KATYA

Tichon, Tichon, never leave me!

Tišo, Tišo, neodjiždej!

Enter Glasha and Feklusha, carrying his luggage.

Will he be long away?	Na dlouho jede?

GLASHA

No, not long.	Ne na dlouho.

Exit with Feklusha.

KATYA

Tichon, never leave me!	Tišo, neodjiždėj!
Oh, my beloved, never leave me!	Holoubku můj! Neodjiždėj!

TICHON

How can I, Katya?	Nelze, Kaťo!
How can I not go when Mama has asked me to?	Jak nepojedu, když maminka posila?

KATYA

Then take me with you, Tichon! Take me too.	Vezmi mne takė s sebou! Vezmi mne!

TICHON

I cannot do that!	Neni to možné!

KATYA

Oh, but why can't you do it?	Proč by to nebylo možné?
So then you love me no more?	Což pak už mne nemáš rád?

TICHON

Love? Yes of course!	Ne, mám tė rád!
But in this kind of slave existence, even a man	Ale z takové otročiny človėk by utekl
with the loveliest wife in the world cannot bear it,	od ženy krasavice nevim jaké,
so when a man has lived all his life as I have done,	A má-li človėk po celý život takhle žit —
he runs away and leaves his wife.	uteče i od ženy!

KATYA

If you say such cruel things,	Jak tė mám pak mit ráda,
oh, how am I still to love you?	když taková slova mluviš?

TICHON

Only words. Only talk.	Slova sem, slova tam!
What am I to make of you?	Kdo se mne zastane?

KATYA
(*in tears*)

Oh, what ever will become of me?	Kam se já ubožka podėju?
Who will protect me?	Kdo se mne zastane?

TICHON

Stop it!	Přestaň!

KATYA
She goes up to her husband and nestles against him.

Tichon, oh, my dear,	Tišo, holoubku,
either stay here with me or let me go with you;	kdybys zůstal doma, nebo mne vzal s sebou,
I would love you so warmly, love you so tenderly.	tolik bych tė mėla ráda, tak bych tė laskala!
Tichon, don't leave me here without you.	Tišo, komu mne tady necháš?

TICHON

I don't understand you, Katya! I have never seen you act so strangely before. Why now?	Nevyznám se v tobě, Káto! Jindy člověk slova z tebe nedostane — a teď?

KATYA

Tichon don't leave me here alone.	Tišo, komu mne zanecháš?

TICHON

You know I cannot help it. It's no use complaining.	Vždyť víš, že jinak nelze. Jaká tedy pomoc?

KATYA

If you go, something dreadful will happen. Something will happen. D'you know what you must do? Make me swear an oath to you — a terrible oath.	Tišo, stane se bez tebe neštěstí! Stane se neštěstí. Víš tedy, co? Žádej ode mne nějakou strašlivou přísahu!

TICHON

What kind of oath?	Jakou přísahu?

KATYA

Yes, make me swear that while you are gone on your journey I will never for any reason either speak to a stranger or even look at one. That I will never dare to think of another man, but only you, Tichon.	Nu takovou: že za tvoji nepřitomnosti Za žádnou cenu s nikým cizím ani nepromluvim, nikoho nespatřim, že ani pomysliti neopovážim se, Kromě na tebe.

TICHON

But why should I? Why should I?	Ale nač to? nač to?

KATYA

Do just this one thing for me, set my soul at rest.	Pro pokoj mojí duše, prokaž mi tu milost!

TICHON

How could anyone keep such promises?	Jak pak můžeš za sebe ručit?

KATYA
(kneeling)

May I never see my mother or see my father again; may no priest absolve me when I die, if I should . . .	Abych ani otce, ani matky vícekrát nespatřila; abych bez pokání umřela, jestliže —

TICHON
(lifting her to her feet)

How can I? How can I? It is a terrible sin.	Nu, copak? Co děláš? Vždyť je to takový hřich.

KABANICHA
(off stage)

It is time, Tichon.	Je čas, Tichone.

She enters.

It is time, the carriage is at the gate. Everything is ready now.	Nu tak, všecko je hotovo, koně už dojely.

TICHON

I know Mama, now it is time to go!	Ano, prosim, bude čas, maminko.

Well then, why are you waiting?   Nu tak, copak stojíš?

What are your wishes?   Co poroučíte?

Don't you know what's proper? Tell your wife   Copak neznáš pořádku? Nařiď ženě
how she should behave herself while you are absent.   jak se chovat za tvé nepřítomnosti.

I have no need to tell her that.   Však ona jistě sama ví . . .

I want no excuses.   Žádné omlouvání!
Give your orders clearly   Rychle nařizuj,
So I too can hear just what you tell her;   abych i já slyšela, co nařizuješ,
and then when you're back home   a pak, až se vrátíš,
you can find out how well she's obeyed them.   zeptáš se jí, zda všecko splnila.

Do just what Mother says.   Poslouchej maminku!

Make it clear she must always respect me.   Řekni jí, aby nebyla hrubá!

And respect her.   Nebuď hrubá . . .

And must honour me as she would her own mother.   Aby ctila tchyni jak rodnou matku —

Katya, honour Mama as you would your own mother.   Káťo, cti matičku jako rodnou matku.

And not sit about all the time with her hands in her lap.   Ať nesedí se založenýma ručičkama.

And be sure to help Mama while I am absent.   Pracuj něco za moji nepřítomnosti.

And not stare out of the window.   Ať nebloumá očima z oken.

Oh, but Mama.   Ale maminko!

Say it all.   Bude to?

Don't look out of the window.   Nedívej se z oken.

And keep her eyes off other men.   Ať po mladých lidech nekouká.

Oh, but Mama dear, how can I?   Ale maminko, na mou duši!

KABANICHA

What's all the fuss about?	Jen žadné okolky!
It's just as well to say everything.	Je lépe všechno přikazat!

TICHON

| Keep your eyes off other men. | Nedivej se na mladiky. |

Katya breaks down.

KABANICHA

| And now have a word together. | A teď si spolu promluvte! |

Exit.

TICHON

| Are you angry with me? | Hněváš se na mne? |

KATYA

| No. Goodbye. | Ne. S Bohem! |

KABANICHA
(returning with Varvara and Glasha)

Now Tichon, it is time. God be with you.	Nu, Tichone, už maš čas. Jeď, s Bohem!

She sits down.

| Sit down all of you. | Sedněte všichni! |
| God be with you. | Nuž s Bohem. |

She rises, the others likewise. Tichon approaches her.

| Kneel. Kneel. | K nohám, k nohám! |

She points to the ground. Tichon bows down to his knees, then kisses his mother.

TICHON

| Mama, God be with you. | S Bohem, maminko! |

KABANICHA

| Say goodbye to her. | Se ženou se rozluč! |

Katya throws her arms around Tichon's neck.

| Shameless girl! He's not your lover! | Nestydatá! Loučiš se s milencem? |

TICHON

| Goodbye Varvara. Goodbye Glasha. | S Bohem sestřičko, s Bohem Glašo! |

He hurries off.

Marie Slorach in the title role and Barbara Walker as Varvara in the 1983 production of 'Katya Kabanova' at Opera North; producer, Graham Vick; designer, Stefanos Lazaridis (photo: Colin Gordon)

Act Two

Scene One. *Working alcove set back from a room at the Kabanovs'. Late afternoon. Kabanicha, Katya and Varvara sit at their embroidery.*

KABANICHA

There now! You're always boasting
how you love your husband.
Most wives if they are good wives, when
they see their husbands off,
stay in their room for the rest of the day,
sobbing their their hearts out.
But all this, what's it to you?

Vida, chvástala jsi se,
jak máš muže ráda!
Jiná pořádná žena, když muže doprovodí,

půl druhé hodiny naříká,
na podsíni leží.
Ale ty, jakoby nic!

KATYA

Well, I am what I am.
I am not that kind of woman.
Why should I weep so that others can see
me?

Neni proč! Neni proč!
Ani toho nedovedu.
Proč pak bych měla být na posměch lidem?

KABANICHA

If you really loved your husband,
then you would have learnt to weep for
him.
And if you cannot do it
you might at least pretend a little.
It would look better so.
But you don't want to be like the others.
I'm going. See that I'm not disturbed.

Kdybys měla muže ráda,
naučila by ses tomu!

A když to nedoveděš,
kdyby ses aspoň pokusila.
Bylo by slušnější.
Svět nezná ted než pletky a nesvár!
Půjdu! Nevyrušujte mě!

Exit.

VARVARA
(adjusting her head-scarf)

It's so warm indoors —
Glasha will make up our beds in the garden.
You know the gate by the summerhouse?
Mother has locked it and taken the key
away.
And she's hidden it, hidden it, so she
imagines.
I've put another one where I found it,
so that she would not notice it.
If I should see him
I'll tell him: come to the gate and she'll be
waiting.

Půjdu též se projit.
Glaša nám ustele v zahradě.
Za malinami jsou vrátka;
maminka vždycky je zavirá na zámek

a klíč schovává — schovává!

Vzala jsem si ho a dala misto něho jiný,
aby si toho nevšimla.
Uvidím-li ho,
řeknu mu, aby přišel k vrátkům.

She offers Katya the key.

KATYA

But why?

Nač to?

She refuses to take it.

I don't want it. Keep it.

Neni třeba! Nechci!

VARVARA

You say you don't want it — might come in
handy.
Take it, it won't bite you.

Tobě neni třeba a mně se hodi.

Jen si ho vem, však tě neukousne!

KATYA

Why are you tempting me, you shameless
girl?
Have you thought what you are doing?

Cos to natropila, ty svůdnice!

Cožpak je to možné?

101

	(aside)
She must be crazy! Really quite crazy.	Zbláznila jsi se, opravdu zbláznila!

I can't stop all the night talking.	Nemiluju mnoho řeči.
I've other things to do.	Nemám teď na to kdy.

She runs off.

KATYA
(her eyes fixed on the key she is holding)

Here's the key. Sin and shame! How can I escape from evil?	Vida! Neštěstí! Tady je to neštěstí!

(rushing to the window)

Throw it away. Throw it away in the river.	Zahodit klíč! Zahodit daleko do vody.
So I may never see it again.	Abych ho nikdy nenašla!
It burns my hand, burns me like fire.	Pálí mne jako žhavý uhel.
Someone's coming here.	Někdo přichází!

She hurriedly hides the key.

KABANICHA
(off stage, to Dikoy)

If you've got business, then behave yourself.	Přišel-lis s něčím, pak mluv pořádně!
Don't shout!	Nekřič!

KATYA

No, no, no-one! And my heart was beating so fast.	Ne, ne! Nikdo. Tak mi srdce přestalo bít!
No, no-one! Why should it frighten me so?	Ne, nikdo! Jak jsem se polekala!
Why did I hide the key?	A klíč jsem schovala.
I know now. Fate has willed it.	Je vidět, osud tomu chce!
And where is the sin	A jaký pak hřích,
in taking one look at him from afar off?	když na něho pohlédnu — třeba zdaleka?
Perhaps say a word to him,	Třeba s ním pohovořím,
there could not really be any harm in it.	to všecko není ještě neštěstí!
What am I saying? I am lying to myself.	Ale co mluvím, čím se obelhávám?
Even though it kill me,	Ať si třeba zemru,
I've got to see him — I will see him.	jen když ho uvidím! Jen uvidím!
Live or die, I must see Boris!	Buď jako buď, uvidím Borise!
Oh, how I wish it were night!	Jen kdyby už byla noc!

Exit, throwing a shawl over her shoulders. Kabanicha comes into the main room with a lamp; Dikoy follows. The room is now light, the alcove in darkness.

DIKOY

It's nothing much. You see, I'm just a little drunk.	Nic zvláštního, jenom jsem trochu nachmelen.

KABANICHA

Then sleep it off.	Tedy jdi spát!

DIKOY

And where shall I go?	A kam mám jít?

KABANICHA

Go home. Where else?	Domů! Kam bys šel?

DIKOY

If I don't want to go home?	Ale když nechci domů!

KABANICHA

Well, what do you want then? Tell me that.	Nu, čeho si přeješ ode mne?

DIKOY

Listen! I'll tell you.	Hned ti to povím!
Speak to me harshly. It's good for my soul when you treat me harshly.	Domluv mi přece, aby moje srdce se uklidnilo.
You, you alone understand me, the others all hate me so.	Ty jediná v celém městě mne dovedeš rozebrat.

KABANICHA

I suppose they've asked you for money.	Chtěli na tobě zase peněz?

DIKOY

Money, money! Always money!	Dám, dám! Ale nedám!
If you mention money it's as if, as if my belly was all on fire, on fire.	Mukneš o penězích, nic jinak, nic jinak, jak bys mi vnitřnosti pálil!

KABANICHA

You have no-one to cross you. That's why you're a bully.	Nemáš nad sebou staršich, Proto si troufáš!

DIKOY

Bully, am I?	Mlč kmotra!
Listen! This is how it happens.	Kdysi — o velikém postě —
It was during Lent once, just after confession,	kál jsem se a postil, kál jsem se a postil,
A peasant came up and spoke to me —	v tom nějaká nečistá síla
must have been the Devil who prompted him, —	namane mi mužika do cesty.
said he'd come for money that I owed him.	Dřívi vozil, pro peníze přišel.
Satan surely sent him there to tempt me.	Čert ho pro hřích v takou dobu přines'!
Then I sinned.	Zhřešil jsem!
Swore at him and all but thrashed him.	Nadal jsem mu, div neztloukl.
And now see what my heart's like.	Vidiš, jaké mám srdce!

(sidling closer to Kabanicha)

Then after that I begged his forgiveness.	Potom jsem ho prosil za odpuštěni,
I went down on my knees to him.	k nohám jsem se mu sklánět.
Now you see what my heart's really like.	Vidiš, kam mne až srdce přivádí,
You can see just how weak and soft I am.	Vidiš, kam mne až srdce přivadí!

(falling at Kabanicha's feet)

On my knees in the mud before a peasant!	V blátě na zemi jsem k nohám padl!
Kneeling! Oh!	V blátě! Oh!

(whining)

KABANICHA
(pushing Dikoy away)

That's enough! Calm yourself!	Posaď se! Nemuč se!
You should learn better manners!	Ale dbej dobrých mravů, dobrých mravů!

Scene Two. *Night. A steep bank, overgrown; above, the Kabanovs' garden fence and gate. A path leads down the slope.*

KUDRYASH
(with guitar)

Nobody here yet!	Nikoho tu neni!
Then I'll sing a song while I'm waiting.	To si zazpíváme z dlouhé chvíle...
'One day early by the river Walked a lovely maiden.	'Po zahrádce děvucha již Ráno procházela,
Came a young and handsome suitor With rich presents laden.	Na své líce do potoka Často pohlížela!
Fur-lined shoes and silken 'kerchieves For a maiden's pleasure,	Chodí za ni, chodí za ni, šohajíček švarný.
Rings of gold and blood-red rubies, Worth a rich man's treasure.	Drahé dárky kupované Vždy on nosi za ni.
"Take these gifts your true love brings you" Vainly he besought her.	Za dukáty za červené Svoje dárky voli,

103

She gazed only at her image
Mirrored in the water.'

She's not here yet? What's keeping her
there?

He sits down.

'Take your rings and take your rubies,
Riches cannot buy me.
I will rise tomorrow early,
To the fields will hie me.
I will pick sweet scented violets,
Thyme and purple clover.
I will make a posy with them
For my own true lover.
Though all day beneath my window,
Though all night you tarry,
You will never be my true love,
You, I'll never marry!'

Enter Boris. Kudryash sees him.

Hallo, so you've come out for a walk as
well!

Sukénky to, šátečky to,
Botečky soboli' . . .

Copak dělá, že nepřichází? . . .

'Ej, půjdu já mladušenka
Na trh pohlédnouti,
A co se mi líbit bude
Koupím na své pouti.
Ej, koupím já, mladušenka,
Voňavé dvě máty
Zasadím já obě máty
Podle svojí chaty.
Nedeptej jich, švarný šohaj,
Pod mýma oknama,
Ne pro tebe sadila já
Ani zalívala!'

Vida, taky si vyšel na toulku!

BORIS

Is that you, Kudryash?

To jste vy, Kudrjáši?

KUDRYASH

Yes, it's me, Boris Grigoryevich!

Ano, Borise Grigorjeviči!

BORIS

And why are you here?

A proč jste tady?

KUDRYASH

I've reasons of my own.
If I hadn't I'd be home in bed.
And what are you doing here?

Já? Patrně mám proč.
Pro nic za nic bych sem nechodil.
A copak vás sem vede?

BORIS

Look, Kudryash, it's like this.

Hleď, Kudrjáši, oč jde!

He looks around furtively.

I'm supposed to be in this place.
So if it's all the same,
would you oblige me by going elsewhere?

Mne je třeba tady zůstat.
Nebyl bych přišel,
kdyby mně nebylo uloženo!

KUDRYASH

But who was it sent you here?

A kdo vám co uložil?

BORIS

It was too dark to see; some girl or other.
Yes, this is the place,
behind the garden of Kabanov's house
where the pathway is.

Nějaká dívka řekla mi na ulici
Abych přišel sem,
na stráň zahrady Kabanových, kde je
pěšinka.

KUDRYASH

You just be warned by me.
Loving like this is utter folly.

Vždyť jsem vás varoval
zamilovtat se nerozvážně!

BORIS

I know, but I can't help loving her.

Ano, to je moje hoře.

KUDRYASH

Although she's married?

Tak do té vdané?

BORIS

Yes.

Ano.

Do you really want to ruin her?	To ji chcete zahubit?

BORIS

Don't try to scare me off.	Prosím tě, nestraš mne!

KUDRYASH

D'you know whether she loves you?	A má ona vás ráda?

BORIS

No, I only met her once at my uncle's home,	Nevím! Pouze jednou jsem ji uviděl u strýce.
but I've seen her at the the the church service.	Jinak vídávám ji v kostele.
Oh, Vanya,	Ach, Kudrjáši,
If you could see her when she's praying —	kdybys ji viděl, jak se modlí,
then she smiles and it's just as if an angel smiled,	jaký andělský úsměv hrá jí na lící!
and shed all around a radiant light!	A z líce jak by světlo zářilo!

KUDRYASH

Yes, that's Kabanov's wife.	To je tedy Kabanová.

BORIS

Yes.	Ano.

KUDRYASH

Be careful. Watch out.	Tak vida, vida!

VARVARA
(coming through the gate, singing)

'Far away my love is gone across the water,	'Za vodou, za vodičkou, můj Váňa stojí.
Far away my love is gone across the water.'	Za vodou, za vodičkou, můj Váňa stojí.'

KUDRYASH
(walking towards Varvara)

'Buying presents for a maid of high degree.	'Tovar nakupuje carevně svojí.
Buying presents for a maid of high degree.'	Tovar nakupuje carevně svojí.'

VARVARA

'I am not a lady, not a rich man's daughter.	'Nech jsem já i děvucha, to z izby temné.
I am not a lady,not a rich man's daughter.'	Nech jsem já i děvucha, to z izby temné.'

KUDRYASH

'Rich or poor man's daughter, I love none but thee,	'To láska zrobila carevnu z tebe.
Rich or poor man's daughter, I love none but thee.'	To láska zrobila carevnu z tebe.'

VARVARA
She walks down the path, her face hidden in her scarf. She goes up to Boris.

Friend, don't get impatient, she's coming.	Ty, mládenče, počkej! Dočkáš se!
(to Kudryash)	
Come to the river.	Pojďme k Volze!

She slips off with Kudryash.

BORIS

This night! Singing! And lovers meeting!	Ta noc! Písně! Dostaveníčko!
And there they go so happily.	Jdou zavěšeni, veseli.
But I wait here, and don't know what I wait for,	Také já čekám. Ale nač čekám.
and I dare not even think about it.	Nevím, ani představit si nedovedu!
Oh, how my heart beats! What am I to say to her?	Srdce mi bije. Nevím, co jí řeknu . . .
She's here!	Tu jde!

Is that you, Katerina Petrovna?	Jste to vy, Katěrino Petrovno?
I don't know how I can ever thank you.	Ani nevím, jak vám děkovati...
Oh, if you knew, Katerina Petrovna,	Ach, kdybyste, Katěrino Petrovno,
Oh, if you only knew	kdybyste věděla,

He tries to take her hand.

how much I love you!	jak vás mám rád, jak vás mám rád!

KATYA

(*without raising her eyes*)

Stay away from me. No, stay away from me.	Nedotýkej se mne, ach nedotýkej se mne!
Leave me here alone.	Jdi ode mne pryč!
You know that I can never atone for my sin,	Vždyť víš, že toho hřichu neodčinim,
never atone for my sin.	nikdy neodčinim.
It lies so heavy on my guilty soul,	Vždyť mi jako kámen pada na duši,
lies so heavy.	jako kámen!

BORIS

Don't send me away,	Neodhanějte mne,
don't send me away so cruelly!	neodhanějte mne od sebe!

KATYA

Why did you come here? Why did you come here?	Proč jsi přišel, proč jsi přišel?
You know I am married	Vždyť jsem vdaná žena,
and until I die must honour and love my husband.	vždyť mám až do hrobu žiti se svym mužem.
So what is it you want then?	Co to na sebe chystám?
You just want my ruin.	Ty chceš moji zkáze!

BORIS

Why should I want your ruin?	Proč bych chtěl vaši zkáze?
When to me you are more than all the world itself.	Když vás miluji víc než všechno na světě!
Yes, to me you are more than all the world itself.	Když vás miluji víc než všechno na světě!

KATYA

D'you want to ruin me, yes ruin me?	Chceš sebe zahubit, nás zahubit?

BORIS

What's your will then?	Vaši vůli!

KATYA

Since I left my home	Že jsem domov opustila,
to come here in the night and secretly,	v noci přišla za tebou...
my own will is abandoned.	nemám svobodné vůle!
If my will were free any longer	Kdybych měla svobodné vůle,
I would not have come to meet you here.	nebyla bych přišla za tebou!
You surely see.	Co nevidiš?

(*raising her eyes and gazing at Boris*)

It is your will conquering my will!	Tvoje vůle nade mnou vládne!
You must surely see!	Což to nevidíš?

She throws her arms around Boris's neck.

Light of my life!	Životě můj!

BORIS

Light of my life.	Životě můj!

They remain in an embrace.

KATYA

Now might I die, and die happy.	Tak se mi zachtělo zemřit...

Why talk of dying . . . now that life is sweet?	Proč pak umírat, když je nám krásně žít?

No, oh, no, I cannot live.	Nikoli, mně nelze žít?

Don't say that! Don't torture me so! Can't you see how much I suffer with you?	Neřikej mi takových slov. Nemuč mne. Což mi tebe není líto?

Why should you suffer? No-one is guilty but I, yes, I alone who brought you here. Kill me but don't pity me! So all may see me, all may know me — the guilty one!	Nač mne litovat? Nikdo není vinen, já sama, sama přišla za tebou. Nelituj mne, zahub mne, ať všichni vědí, co dělám!

You make too much of it. You think too much of it.	Nač na to pomyslet? Nač na to pomyslet?

It is I who have sinned by loving you — Mine the suffering.	Když jsem pro tebe se hříchu dopustila, proč netrpět?

They embrace impetuously.

So you've found each other.	Nuže, shodli jste se?

Yes!	Shodli.

Then go for a stroll. Vanya will call when it's time to go back.	Tak projděte se! Vaňa vás zavolá, až bude třeba.

Exeunt Katya and Boris.

This way, it's ever so much easier. Out by the gate in the garden.	To jste si vymyslili pěknou věc! Lézt skrz zahradní vratka!

He sits down on a rock with Varvara.

Yes, thanks to me.	To všechno já.

So I imagined. But suppose that your mother should find you out?	To je ti podobno. Ale nepřijde-li na to maminka?

Oh, mother will never get round to it. She's a very heavy sleeper.	Eh, ani ji na mysl nepřijde! První spánek bývá tvrdý.

But suppose the devil should wake her just once?	Přece však, pojednou ji čert nedá spát.

Even so. The gate that leads from her room
to ours is always locked at night time.
She will knock and go away.
Next day I'll tell her that we both slept
soundly.
And old Dikoy had come to call on her.
They are such boors — they suit each other
well.

Co na tom? Ze dvora vedou vrátka,
která se zevnitř zavírají.
Bude klepat . . . odejde.
Ráno ji řeknu, že jsme tvrdě spaly.

A pak Dikoj je u ní návštěvou.
Takoví hrubci a rozumějí si!

BORIS
(*in the distance*)

For ever I am yours!

Už dávno jsem tě znal!

KATYA
(*in the distance*)

For ever I am yours!

Už dávno jsem tě znala!

VARVARA

Anyway Glasha is on the look out,
and if there's any danger she'll call us.

Ostatně na stráži stojí Glaša.
Kdyby se něco šustlo, zavolá.

BORIS
(*in the distance*)

Unto the world's far end with you beside
me!

Zdá se mi, že kraj světa šel bych za tebou!

VARVARA

Anyway, where is the fun without some
risk?
If you don't take care then you're in for
trouble.
How are we going to know what the time is?

Ostatně bez nebezpečí to nejde!

Než se naděješ, padneš do neštěstí!

Kdybychom věděli, kolik je hodin?

KUDRYASH

One o'clock!

Jedna!

VARVARA

How d'you know?

Jak víš?

KUDRYASH

Heard the nightwatchman.

Ponocný tloukl . . .

KATYA
(*in the distance*)

Light of my life!
Unto the world's end I will go with you.

Živote můj,
kraj světa šla bych, šla bych za tebou!

BORIS
(*in the distance*)

Light of my life!

Živote můj!

VARVARA

It's time. You'd better call them.

Je čas! Zavolej na ně!

BORIS
(*in the distance*)

For ever light of my life!

Kraj světa, živote můj!

KUDRYASH

'Homeward all good people, homeward all
good people!
But myself I will not go!

'Všecko domů, domů všecko domů.

A já domů nepůjdu!'

BORIS
(*off stage*)

Coming!   Slyším.

KUDRYASH
He and Varvara climb up the path to the gate.

'It is night and far from home   'Choď si divka do času, do večerniho času,
Maidens should no longer roam.
Ei le-li, le-li, le-li, maidens should no   aj, le-li, le-li, le-li, do večerniho času.'
  longer roam.'

VARVARA

'I am young and I am fair,   'A já divka jsem mladá, a já raději do rána,
Stay with me till day is here.
Ei le-li, le-li, le-li, stay with me till day is   Aj, le-li, le-li, le-li, do raníčka do rána.'
  here.'

KUDRYASH

'So we stayed, my love and I,   'A jak zora vstávala,
Till the dawn was in the sky.   Já se domu sebrala,
Ei, le-li, le-li, le-li,   Aj, le-li, le-li, le-li
Till the dawn was in the sky.'   Já se domu sebrala.'

Katya and Boris hurry up the path.

VARVARA
(*calling to them*)

Can't you say goodbye to each other?   Zdalipak se rozloučite?

Katya goes on up the path alone; Boris stays behind.

'Katya Kabanova' at Sadler's Wells in 1951; Marion Studholme as Varvara and Robert Thomas as Kudryash (photo: Angus McBean © Harvard Theatre Collection)

Act Three

A ruined building with colonnades and vaulted ceilings; around it, grass and bushes. Through the arches a view of the Volga and its banks. Late afternoon on a dull day with rain clouds. Kuligin and Kudryash come into the ruin for shelter.

KULIGIN

Raining!	Krápe!

KUDRYASH

There's a storm coming.	Přijde bouře!

KULIGIN

Good, here's a place to shelter.	Dobře, že je kde se schovat!

KUDRYASH

What a crowd there on the promenade!	A co lidu na bulváru!

KULIGIN

You'll see, they will all come rushing in here.	Zdá se, že se všecko nahrne sem!

Passers-by come running in from the rain.

KUDRYASH

Merchants' wives all dressed in their finery.	Kupcové jdou naparádéné.

KULIGIN

You know, this must have been covered with paintings!	A vida! Tady je vymalováno!
Here and there you can see.	Misty je to znát.

(inspecting the walls)

KUDRYASH

Ruined by fire.	Vyhořelo.

KULIGIN

That's a picture of hell and the damned!	Je to Gehenna, pekelný oheň?

KUDRYASH

Afterwards they never restored it.	Po požáru neopravili.

KULIGIN

Every kind of person burning away in there.	Všeho druhu lidé do něho padají.

KUDRYASH

Yes, yes, my friend!	Tak, brachu milý!

KULIGIN

All sorts of people!	Všech důstojnosti!

KUDRYASH

Yes, we all of us come to it.	Tak, tak, dobřes to pochopil.

KULIGIN

There are black men as well there.	Také mouřeninové!

KUDRYASH

Yes! There are black men as well there.	Taky, taky mouřeninové!

Dikoy enters. All the others bow.

DIKOY

Out of the way! I'm soaked to the skin.   Celého mne to pokropilo!

KUDRYASH

Savol Prokofjevich!   Savjole Prokofjiči!

DIKOY

Get away from me, right away!   Odraz ode mne! Odraz!
Cheeky young puppy!   Co na mne lezeš?
I suppose you are after something.   Možná, že nechci s tebou ani mluvit!
Running round me and poking your nose   Přímo rypákem se žene do hovoru!
in my business.

KUDRYASH

We get storms here frequently.   Bouře zde často bývají.

DIKOY

Nonsense!   Nesmysl!

KUDRYASH

We need lightning conductors.   Hromosvodů nemáme!

DIKOY

Nonsense!   Nesmysl!
Well, and what are they like, your lightning   Nu, a jaképak máš ty hromosvody?
conductors?

KUDRYASH

Rods made of steel.   Ocelové!

DIKOY

What else?   Co dál?

KUDRYASH

All made of steel. Long rods.   Ocelové-tyče.

DIKOY

I heard you. Long rods.   Slyšel jsem, že tyče.

KUDRYASH
(*explaining with gestures*)

Fixed to the roof.   Spustí se tyče.

DIKOY

What else? What else?   Co dál? Co dál?

KUDRYASH

That's all.   Nic víc!

DIKOY
(*rolling his sleeves up menacingly*)

What is a storm in your way of reckoning?   A co je bouřka po tvojim rozumu?

KUDRYASH

Just electricity.   Elektřina!

DIKOY
(*stamping his foot*)

Just electricity! Just electricity!   Jakápak elektřina? Jaká elektřina?
There you are. Just a common charlatan.   Vida! Po tom nejsi loupežník?
Storms are sent as a punishment   Bouře je trest na nás,
so that we mortals know God is almighty.   Abychom moc boží pociťovali!
You with your rods of steel   A ty chceš tyčemi nebo rožni nějakými
would defy the fury of the thunder and the   Proti ní se bránit?
lightning!

111

Are we all just heathen? Are we heathen?
Are you?

Co jsi ty? Jsi Tatar? Tatar? Nu mluv!
Tatar?

KUDRYASH

Worthy and honoured sir,
surely you must know the words of our poet:
"My flesh will crumble into dust
But the thunder obeys my will."

Savjole Prokofjiči! Vaše slovutnosti!
Děržavin praví:
"Mé tělo rozpadne se v prach,
Však rozum hromem zvlád'!"

DIKOY

Listen to him! What a thing to say!
Off you go then! You're just a common-
place charlatan.

Velectěni, co to povidal?
Podržte ho! Takový falešný mužiček!

(turning to the bystanders)

As for you, all you good-for-nothings, you
just make trouble.

Darmo, proklatci, člověka ve hřich
uvádite!

(to Kudryash)

Has it stopped raining?

Přestalo pršet?

KUDRYASH

Seems so!

Zdá se.

DIKOY

Seems so!
Go and look for yourself.
And all he says is — 'Seems so'.

Zdá se.
Jdi a podivej se!
A to si řekne: "Zdá se!"

*Dikoy walks out of the building, the rest following. Varvara appears under one of the arches,
looking out into the open.*

KUDRYASH
(still outside)

The rain has stopped.

Přestalo.

In the background, Kudryash accosts Boris.

VARVARA
(making a sign to Boris)

Hey! Boris! It's him, he's back!

Pssst! Pssst! Zdá se, že je to on!

He approaches her.

What are we to do with Katya?

Co si počnem s Katěrinou?

BORIS

Why, what is it?

Co se děje?

VARVARA

Oh, it's awful, her husband came back
today!
Quite unexpected. Surely you knew?

Ale hotové neštěsti! Nic jinak!
Muž se jí vrátil, viš o tom?

BORIS

No!

Nevím!

VARVARA

And she's gone out of her senses.

Ale Katěrina je prostě nesvou!

BORIS

Oh, how can I bear it?

Ach, to jí už nespatřim!

VARVARA

Oh, you! Listen to me now!
She is so pale and shaking as if she'd a fever.
She wanders through the house
not hearing or seeing me,
just like a mad woman,
then suddenly she's sobbing and moaning.

Ach, ty! Poslyš mne přece!
Celá se chvěje, jak by ji zimnice lomcovala!
Je bledá, potáci se po domě
jak by něco hledala!
Oči má jak šilená!
Dnes ráno začala plakat, stále vzlykat:

112

Oh, tell me friend, what am I to do?
She is doing such crazy things.

Ach, batušky! Co si mám počit?
Takových věci natropi.

BORIS

Oh, my God! What can I do?

Ach, bože, co si počit?

VARVARA

And I'm afraid she'll fall down, kneel
before him,
and then blurt out everything.

— že, pravim ti, že prašti sebou o zem
a všechno mu povi.

BORIS

Would she do that?

Je-li možná?

VARVARA

I cannot answer for her.
Mother has begun to notice,
watches like a serpent, watches like a
serpent.
That makes her all the worse.
Here she comes. Mother's close behind her.
Hide yourself!

U ni je všechno možné!
Maminka si toho všimla;
pořád na ni kouká, jako zmije kouká,
a ji je z toho hůř!
Tu jdou! Maminka jde s nimi! Schovej se!

Boris and Kudryash hide. Distant thunder.

KATYA
(rushing in, taking Varvara's hand and gripping it frenziedly)

Oh, Varvara!
I shall die!

Ach, Varvaro!
Moje smrt!

WOMAN
(from the crowd)

Look at that woman! Something has
frightened her.

Nějaká ženská náramně se boji!

VARVARA
(to Katya)

Watch what you're saying.

Nu dosti, dosti!

CHORUS

No-one can run away from the wrath of
God!
Look there! What a beauty!

Co komu souzeno, tomu neuteče!
Vida, krasavice!

VARVARA

Calm yourself!

Vzmuž se!

KATYA

How can I?

Nemohu!

VARVARA

Do be quiet.

Vzpamatuj se!

KATYA

My heart is broken.

Srdce mne boli!

KUDRYASH
(to Boris, who is just behind him)

Don't be afraid, you are safe with us.

Čeho se bojite, prosim vás?

CHORUS

Oh, what a beauty!

Ej, krasavice!

KUDRYASH

Every blade of grass rejoices.
Don't be so sad about it.

Každé kvitko raduje se
A vy se schovávate?

113

KATYA
(seeing Boris)

Ah! Why does he come here?	Ach, co tu ještě chce?

She leans towards Varvara and sobs.

Oh, can he really care so little?	Či je mu toho ještě málo?
Oh, can he really care so little how much I suffer?	Či je mu toho ještě málo, jak já se mučím?

VARVARA

Calm yourself, kneel down, say a prayer.	Utiš se, poklekni, pomodli se.

Enter Dikoy with Kabanicha and Tichon.

DIKOY
(to Kabanicha, pointing at Katya)

Something is troubling that woman's conscience.	Jaké pak může mít zvláštní hříchy?

KABANICHA

No man knows his neighbour's heart.	Cizí duše temnota.

KATYA
(suddenly falling to her knees)

Mama! Tichon!	Maminko! Tichone!
Look on this sinner and pity her!	Hříšná jsem před Bohem, před vámi!
Look on me.	Hříšná jsem!
Ah, did I not swear a solemn oath	Což jsem se vám nezapřisáhla,

(distant thunder)

that I would speak to no man, I would look at no man	že se na nikoho ani nepodívám
while my husband was absent?	za tvé nepřítomnosti?
Would you know then all my wickedness ...	A víš-li, co jsem, nemravná,
What I did when you left me that very night ...	bez tebe udělala? Hned první noc ...

TICHON

No, I won't listen.	Mlč, není třeba!

VARVARA

She doesn't mean it.	Neví, co mluví.

KATYA

I left the house.	... jsem z domu utekla ...

KABANICHA

Go on then, say what you have to say.	No, mluv, mluv, když jsi už začala!

KATYA

That night and every night I spent with him —	... a celých deset nocí s ním se toulala.

KABANICHA

Who?	S kým?

DIKOY

Who?	S kým?

KABANICHA

Who?	S kým?

VARVARA

No, she is lying, she doesn't mean it.	Vždyť ona lže — neví, co mluví.

KATYA

Boris Grigoryevich!   S Borisem Grigorjičem!

Thunder. She falls senseless into her husband's arms.

KABANICHA

Son, your mother warned you!   Synku, dočkal jsi se!

TICHON

Katerina!   Katěrino!

Thunder. Katya tears herself away and rushes off into the storm. The rest run in all directions.

Scene Two. *A lonely spot on the bank of the Volga. Dusk, turning to night.*

TICHON
(*followed by Glasha, running with a lamp and looking everywhere*)

Ah! Glasha! It's awful to think of it!   Ach Glašo! Co může být horšiho?
Did you hear mother tell us: to kill her is   Utlouci ji to je málo!
  not enough —
women like her should be buried alive.   Maminka povídá: "Do země za živa ji
                zakopat,
The least you could do is beat her.   aby svou vinu smyla!"
But I'm fond of her still.   Ale já ji mám rád;
Oh, how could I then do anything to harm   lito je mi jenom prstem se ji dotknout.
  her?

GLASHA
(*running after Tichon*)

Katerina!   Katěrino!

She rushes off. Enter Kudryash in haste, followed by Varvara.

VARVARA

Mother started shouting at me   Na zámek mne zavírá, týrá,
so I told her — Leave me alone.   řekla jsem jí: "Nezavírejte mne!
Something bad will happen, something   Bude zle! Bude zle! Bude zle!"
  bad, something bad, something bad.
Tell me, friend, what shall I do?   Pouč mne, jak mám teď žít?

KUDRYASH

Come away. Yes, come with me.   Jak žít? Teď utéci!

VARVARA

Go with you?   Utéci?

KUDRYASH

Let's go to Moscow.   V Moskvu matičku?

VARVARA

Moscow, away to a new life!   V nový veselý život!

They run off together.

TICHON
(*from a distance*)

Katerina!   Katěrina!

GLASHA
(*from a distance*)

Katerina!   Katěrina!

Katya enters slowly from the other side.

KATYA

No! Nobody here, then! Oh, where can he   Ne! Nikdo tu neni! Co as chudák dělá?
  be now?

115

If I saw him once again I would die happy.
I should have borne my sin in silence,
but I let him suffer with me
and brought shame and ruin on him.
Yes, shame and ruin on myself and him
    too!

Vidět se s nim, rozloučit, pak třeba zemřit!
Vždyť mi tim neni ulehčeno!
Tak jsem sebe zahubila,
sebe o čest připavila!
Ano! Sebe o čest, jemu pokořeni!

KULIGIN
(*just off stage, back*)

La-la-la-la la-la

La-la-la!

La-la-la-la-la-la

He crosses the stage, peering at Katya.

La-la-la

KATYA
(*shrinking*)

I've forgotten how he would speak to me,
how he'd look at me — all forgotten.
And the nights — oh, how I feel it!
And then the world lies sleeping,
the whole world.
But I shall not sleep again in this life.
I dread the darkness.
I am afraid.

Vzpomenu si, jak ke mně hovořil?
Jak mne miloval? Nevzpomenu!
Ach, ty noci, jak jsou mi těžké!
Všichni jdou spat tak lehce.
I ja jdu.
Ale jak bych se do mohyly kladla.
Ta hrůza potmě!
Nějaky hluk!

Chorus in the distance, wordless.

KATYA

And there's singing too.

A to zpívani!

Chorus as before.

Far in the distance like funeral chanting!
Oh, I am so glad when daylight comes
    again.

Jako by někoho pochovávali!
A člověk je rád, když konečně je světlo!

A drunkard crosses the stage, staring at her.

Why does he stare at me?
Long ago for sins like mine they would kill
    a woman.
Women like me were taken and thrown in
    the river.
But I must live, live!
Live, live! Atone for all my sinning.
Why must I suffer so?
How long shall I have to suffer?
What more can I live for now? What?
What more? No, I want nothing more.
    Nothing can make me happy.
Even the golden sunshine cheers me no
    longer.
But death comes not to me.
Though I call him, still death comes not to
    me.
All I can see around me, all I can hear
    around me
only hurts me, hurts me here so badly.

Proč se tak chovaji?
Řika se, že takové ženské zabijeli!

Kdyby mne tak vzali a hodili do Volhy!

Ale tak-žij, žij,
žij, žij! a muč se se svym hřichem!
Však už jsem zmučena!
A dlouho-li mám se mučit?
Nu, nač mám tu ještě žit? Nu?
Nu nač? Nic nepotřebuji. Nic mi neni
    milo.
Ani to boži světlo mi neni milo.

Ale smrt nepřichazi.
Toužiš po ni: ona nepřichazi.

Ať vidim cokoli, ať slyšim cokoli,

jenom tady, tady to boli!

(her hand to her heart)

Ah, if I could live with him,
perhaps then I might find some
    happiness . . .
but if I may not see him,
then let him hear me calling, hear me
    calling from far away.
Oh, mighty stormwind,
bear my grief and longing to my love!
Oh, I am so sad and weary!

Snad, kdybych s nim mohla žit,
bych ještě nějakou radost zažila.

Když tě už neuvidim,
kdybys aspoň zdáli mne uslyšel!

Vy větry bujné!
Doneste mu žalostny můj stesk!
Ach batušky, styska se mi!

She approaches the steep bank.

Light of my life, joy of my soul!
Dearest heart, oh, how I love you!

Živote můj, radosti moje,
duše má, jak tě mám ráda!

116

Enter Boris. At first he does not see her.

Answer me! Oh, answer me!   Ozvi se! Ach, ozvi se!

That is her calling me.   Vždyť je to její hlas!

KATYA

Answer me! Oh, answer me!   Ozvi se, ach, ozvi se!

She runs up to Boris.

BORIS

Katya!   Kato!

They fall into each other's arms.

KATYA AND BORIS

Now once again I see you!   Přece tě ještě vidim!

Katya weeps on his breast; they remain locked together in an embrace. Then awareness returns.

BORIS

Thanks be to God!   Svedl nás Bůh!

KATYA

You have not forgotten me?   Nezapomněls na mne?

BORIS

Forget you, my dearest! How could I?   Jak bych měl zapomnět, co mysliš?

KATYA

No, no! It was something else I wanted to tell you.   Ne, ne! Chtěla jsem něco jineho řici.

Then you do not hate me?   Nezlobiš se na mne?

BORIS

Ah, how could I hate you?   Proč bych se měl zlobit?

KATYA

I never meant any harm.   Nechtěla jsem tvého zla!
Surely I had lost my senses   Nebyla jsem sebe mocna,
when I told them everything.   když jsem všechno prozradila.
No, not that! No, not that! It was something else I wanted to tell you.   Ale ne, ale ne! Chtěla jsem ti něco jineho řici.

(coming suddenly back to the present)

But what of you now? Tell me that.   Co budeš dělat? Co s tebou?

BORIS

My uncle has told me I must go away,   Strýc mne vyháni až na Sibiř!
leave this town for ever.   Do obchodu v Kjachtě!

KATYA

Then take me with you. Ah, no!   Vezmi mne s sebou! Ach ne!
Go, and forget that you knew me.   Jeď s Bohem, netrap se pro mne.

BORIS

It's easier for a man.   Což já jsem volný pták.
I shall be free to do as I wish.   Což bych já o sobě uvažoval!
But you ... What of Kabanicha, what will she do?   Ale co bude s tebou? Co s tchyni?

KATYA

Mother will torture me —   Mučí mne, zavirá ...
and the people will stare at me   na mne všichni se divaji,
when I go through the streets,   do oči se mi směji,
mocking and laughing at me.   tebe mi vyčitaji ...

BORIS

And your husband? — A co tvůj muž?

KATYA

Sometimes he is gentle, then he gets angry, drinks — and beats me. — Chvílemi je laskav, hned se zas zlobí. Pije! Mne bije!

No, not that! All the time I'm thinking other things. — Ale ne. Vždyť mluvím stále něco jiného!

It was something else I wanted to tell you. — Chtěla jsem ti něco jiného říci.

I was so sick with longing for you, — Stýskalo se mi po tobě.

and now, now at last I see you once again. — A hle, nyní jsem tě opět uviděla!

Listen, listen . . . something I had to tell you . . . — Počkej, počkej, co jsem ti chtěla říci . . .

Everything is confused. — V hlavě se mi to plete . . .

BORIS

I must go. — Už mám čas!

KATYA

I can no longer remember it. — Na nic si nemohu vzpomenout.

Wait a moment and I'll tell you. — Počkej, hnedle ti to povím!

When you have left me, — Až půjdeš cestou,

give alms to each beggar you meet with. — dej každému žebráku almužnu,

Ask them to pray for my soul. — žádného neopomeň!

The Chorus intones a vowel between U and O, like the Volga sighing. Complete darkness.

KATYA

And for the last time look in my eyes as I gaze into yours. — A nyní dej se na sebe podívat naposledy!

What is that song they sing? — Co to zpívají?

So go now, goodbye. God bless you! — Buď s Bohem! Nuž jdi! Buď s Bohem!

BORIS

Oh, if they only knew how cruel parting is! — O kdyby věděli, jak těžko se loučím!

How cruel parting is! How cruel parting is! — Jak těžko se loučím! Jak těžko se loučím!

(as he walks away)

Cruel! — Těžko!

KATYA

And still I hear that song. — A ještě zpívají

(crawling on hands and knees to the edge of the bank)

Birds will sing as they fly above me — ptáčci přiletí na mohylu,

where I am buried, — vyvedou mláďata,

and flowers will blossom there, purple flowers, — a kvítka vykvetou, červeňoučká,

blue flowers, yellow flowers. — modroučká, žluťoučká.

So peaceful, so lovely, — Tak ticho, tak krásně, Tak krásně!

so lovely, and I must die! — A třeba umřít!

She crosses her arms and leaps into the river.

KULIGIN
(on the far bank)

Ho there, a woman has jumped in the river! — Nějaká ženská skočila do vody!

PASSER-BY
(on the far bank)

Ho, bring a boat! — Hej — loďku sem!

DIKOY
(rushing past with a lantern)

Who's that calling? — Kdo to volá?

GLASHA	
Ho, bring a boat!	Hej — loďku sem!

TICHON

Here! Quickly, come quickly!	O baťušky baťušky!

People rush up with lanterns from all sides.

It surely must be her.	To je jisté ona!

Kabanicha enters, following Dikoy. She grabs hold of Tichon.

Let me go!	Pusťte mne!

KABANICHA

No, my son!	Nepustím!
Let her alone. She isn't worth it.	Stálo by za to sebe zničit!

TICHON

You are the one who killed her.	Vy jste ji zahubila,
You, yes, and you alone.	vy, vy jen samotná!

KABANICHA

What's this? Are you quite crazy?	Co ty? Nejsi při smyslech!
Don't speak to me like that!	Neviš, s kým mluvíš?

Dikoy enters carrying Katya's corpse. He lays it on the ground.

DIKOY

Here's your Katerina for you!	Zde máte svou Katěrinu.

Exit in agitation.

TICHON
(flinging himself on the body and sobbing)

Katya! Katya!	Káto! Káto!

KABANICHA

I must thank you, I must thank you,	Děkuji vám, děkuji vám,
friends and neighbours,	dobří lidé,
for your kindness.	za úslužnost!

She bows to this side and that. The Chorus intones wordlessly as before.

*Katya's body is pulled from the Volga at the end of David Pountney's Scottish Opera
production, designed by Maria Bjørnson (photo: Eric Thorburn)*

119

Act One of 'Jenůfa' at Covent Garden in 1956, with Edith Coates as Grandmother Buryja and Amy Shuard in the title role (photo: Houston Rogers, Theatre Museum)

Janáček's Operas — Preparation and Performance

Charles Mackerras

Charles Mackerras first came into contact with Janáček's operas in Prague in 1947, when he heard his teacher Václav Talich conduct 'Katya Kabanova'. He was overwhelmed by the performance and later during his time in Czechoslovakia he managed to hear most of Janáček's other operas. On his return to Britain he persuaded Sadler's Wells Opera to mount 'Katya Kabanova', conducting its British première on April 10, 1951. In later years he conducted most of Janáček's operas for SWO/English National Opera, 'Jenůfa' for The Royal Opera and several of the other operas all over the world, including Czechoslovakia. He has recorded five Janáček operas for Decca with the Vienna Philharmonic Orchestra, and has had published editions of 'The Makropulos Case' and 'Katya Kabanova'.

During my Janáček-conducting career I have very much altered my view of what changes should be made to the scores for performances. I started off with the idea that because Janáček was such an eccentric he needed a lot of 'help' in order to get his music appreciated by the normal opera-going public. In recent years, just as I have become a little more strict about what I consider authentic style in the performance of Handel and other Baroque music, I have become more unbending about keeping to what Janáček actually wrote. It seems to have been my fate to become interested in the two most terrible writers-down of music in history: I cannot imagine any composer whose intentions are harder to discover from the way they wrote than Janáček and Handel. With Janáček, once you have learned to decipher the funny way he writes, you see that the sounds are what he intended — the strange things are not mistakes or the result of amateurism.

When I first heard *Katya Kabanova* it was performed in Václav Talich's version which, although I did not know it at the time, reorchestrated the work to beautify and normalise it. I just drank in the marvellous music and the wonderful atmosphere of the whole opera. But I quickly realised that other Janáček operas which I heard in Prague did sound different. I assumed that was simply because they were different operas. At that time, of course, *Jenůfa* was only performed in the orchestration by Karel Kovařovic, and *From the House of the Dead* was performed in an orchestration by Janáček's pupils, Břetislav Bakala and Osvald Chlubna. When I heard *Katya Kabanova* performed elsewhere in Czechoslovakia it sounded rather different from the Prague performances. I realised that some changes had been made to the orchestration, but I did not know how far-reaching they were until I came to prepare the work for Sadler's Wells. Then I discovered there were also many things wrong with the parts, which I tried to make sense of. Later I worked on *The Makropulos Case* and realised that things were wrong there as well. I felt so passionate about these works that I determined to get to the bottom of the problems and find out what the differences were and why they were there. At the invitation of the Czech government I spent a long time going round the places where Janáček worked, and studying the original sources to see the extent of the difficulty in producing proper texts of his music.

The materials

One of the problems is that Janáček's writing down of his music was so untidy that it can be very difficult to tell what he wanted. This caused his copyists to make mistakes and, because his proof-reading was so slap-dash and haphazard, he would pass a work as properly corrected in accordance with his wishes when it was actually still full of mistakes. Some of these are quite far-reaching: for example, in the last movement of the Sinfonietta the tremendous cymbal crash, which sets off the reappearance of the brass band, is in the wrong place.

But the problems do go back farther than this. Janáček was unconventional and, even when he wrote down what he wanted, people thought he must have meant something else. He wrote things down in a terrible way — sometimes he would write a phrase with the norm being a crotchet and then with the norm being a quaver, and it can be very hard to tell if he wanted a different tempo suddenly or whether it was just a different way of writing the same thing. He also seemed to have a fixation about writing music in flat keys, which makes some passages very difficult for string players. But when he then goes into certain extreme keys, because he never wrote a key signature, he starts writing double flats and gets into a situation where certain quite simple chords end up with extremely complicated notation.

Some people try to change all that and ask, Why not rewrite the works so that they are more easily readable for the ordinary musician? There are musicologists who have added key signatures and changed Janáček's methods of writing rhythms in order to make them more immediately clear to the players. But this does raise questions about how far one is justified in making changes to the look of a score so as to make it more accessible to the players. I rather sit on the fence about this. As a conductor I do find myself irritated by the way that quite simple rhythmic concepts are made terribly difficult to grasp because of the way in which Janáček wrote them down, and in my own sets of orchestral parts I certainly do change the rhythmic patterns to suit the way *I* believe they should be played. But this is only my personal viewpoint and when Universal Edition engaged me to edit first *Katya Kabanova* and then *The Makropulos Case*, I found that many of the things I would do in performance came under the heading of *my* interpretation of what I *think* Janáček wanted, which raises questions in producing a published edition of a composer — especially a composer like Janáček who wrote things down so eccentrically. How much is the editor allowed to interpret? — which is still more of a problem when, as in my case, the editor is an interpreter anyway. In the case of *Katya Kabanova* I have tried to be meticulous about what the original is and what is simply my opinion of how it should be performed. In my edition of *The Makropulos Case*, I started off by doing a lot of interpretation and then rather repented of it, so I have now changed quite a lot of my edition. The case of *From the House of the Dead* is rather different. There is so little to go on because, although Janáček completed the piece before he died, he did not have time to have the fair copy of the score made and corrected. Many people have had a go at producing the original version — Rafael Kubelik was one of the first to try, and there have been at least three others in Czechoslovakia as well as myself. But almost any conductor who is vaguely expert in Janáček could produce his own version of the original because the choices are so wide open.

Where does this leave the general musician who does not want to do all the research but expects to be given a score and to get on with it? In the case of

Katya Kabanova a conductor can do just that because my published edition is pretty well fool-proof except for anyone who has as detailed a knowledge of the minutiae as I have and who therefore might make some different choices. I think my edition of *The Makropulos Case* is serviceable in the same way, now that I have revised it. The decisions in *From the House of the Dead* are so variable that the publisher is prepared to let anyone have a go at producing a further version if they believe they can improve on the existing versions — provided they pay for it themselves! Both *The Cunning Little Vixen* and *Mr Brouček* are, amazingly enough, normally written — they have their eccentricities but there are few doubts about what the composer wanted. With *Jenůfa*, however, there are problems because three versions exist. Universal Edition published a score which was a genuine attempt to rid the work of all the errors in the parts and vocal scores — demonstrably wrong notes and so on. They produced a version which tidied all that up and which included the emendations made by great conductors like Talich and Erich Kleiber. But in fact it was a critical edition of Kovařovic's reorchestration — it was rather like producing a score correcting the mistakes in Rimsky-Korsakov's arrangement of *Boris Godunov*!

The three versions of *Jenůfa* are, first, the original as performed in Brno in 1904; second, Janáček's own revision of the original version, as published in the vocal score of 1908 (the changes are mainly cutting repetitions and shortening ensembles); and third, Kovařovic's reorchestration and further cutting for the Prague production of 1916. Kovařovic, who was the artistic director of the National Theatre, had long resisted suggestions that *Jenůfa* should be performed there; in his view such a work might be suitable for provincial Brno, but it was not acceptable in Prague. When he finally bowed to the pressure from the Nationalists to stage the work, it was only on condition that he himself reorchestrated it. He was very much the professional conductor and composer who knew how to orchestrate in what was the accepted fashion — like Elgar, Strauss, Puccini or Ravel.

The original version was not a great artistic success, in part because the orchestra could not really play the music. Janáček, who was a very passionate man, tore up his score but a copy does exist in Vienna and it would be possible to perform this version. In the revised version Janáček made cuts and it is this second version (with two exceptions) which I recorded for Decca. I kept in the original Act One narration for the Kostelnička which Janáček himself cut out. I think it works very well on record but, although I have included it in stage performances, I do understand the argument that it holds up the action at a vital moment. On record I also included the overture which Janáček later arranged as the concert overture *Jealousy*. Even with the original orchestration there is a case for not doing the overture in the theatre but beginning with the amazing mill-wheel effect of the xylophone.

There is a very useful Czech edition of the vocal score made by the musicologist Kašlík, which shows the cuts made by Janáček in his revision and, in different type, the cuts made by Kovařovic. There are also indications of the two orchestrations. But until the Czech State Publishing House, which is producing a complete edition of Janáček, publishes *Jenůfa* in the original orchestration, any conductor who takes on the work faces the task of doing all the musicological work for himself — unless he performs the Kovařovic version. Not every conductor has time to do that, and I worked on the piece for several years to produce my own performing materials of Janáček's orchestration — I can remember entire holidays being spent pasting strips of manuscript paper over Kovařovic's additional instrumentation. I introduced the changes into performances gradually. For example, when I conducted the work in Australia I had a copyist working during the run so that at each performance we got a little nearer to what Janáček wrote. When I conducted *Jenůfa* at the Paris Opéra in 1980 we were able to do virtually the complete original version, except for the ending.

The ending of the opera is something of a special problem. There is a copyist's score of the original version in Brno which has Kovařovic's additions written in red ink by Kovařovic himself. So it is possible to tell with 100 per cent accuracy what Janáček wrote and what Kovařovic wrote — until the final scene. There Kovařovic decided to make so many changes that eventually he wrote the scene out completely in his own version. His ending was rather more triumphant and Wagnerian than Janáček's original conception. The two men did discuss this, and Janáček eventually rather grudgingly agreed that Kovařovic's version was quite good. Janáček's own ending is less optimistic and recognises that Jenůfa and Laca still have problems to face. I believe this ending has a very great deal of validity if produced in a certain way.

When I conduct *Jenůfa* in Vienna we use the Kovařovic version. There is nothing wrong with it except that you have to regard it like Rimsky-Korsakov's version of *Boris Godunov* or Mozart's version of *Messiah*: both are fine works because those are great musicians — but they are different works.'I just wish I could persuade the Vienna State Opera to put in its programme 'Orchestrated by Kovařovic'!

Kerstin Meyer as Kostelnička in the Royal Opera of Stockholm production of 'Jenůfa' (photo: Enar Merkel Rydberg)

Performance

After the musicological work has been done, the conductor of a Janáček opera is basically in the position of a conductor faced with any score. There are special difficulties, but they are no longer quite so difficult as they used to be. I will never forget first trying to do *Katya Kabanova* with the Sadler's Wells Orchestra in 1951. At the end of Act Two, scene two, there is that marvellous double love duet: the music has the most remarkable sounds, with the second violins playing harmonics four octaves higher than the double basses, which are divided into five parts. But, instead of sounding evocative of a hot night on the banks of the Volga, it was indescribably ghastly — and that was played by quite a good orchestra. Remembering this makes me realise why *Jenůfa* must have sounded so dreadful in Brno all those years ago and why Kovařovic thought he needed to re-orchestrate it. When I came to conduct *Katya Kabanova* at the London Coliseum in 1973, however, there were about three members of the orchestra remaining who had played in the 1951 performances. I remember them saying to me how difficult the music had seemed in 1951, whereas 22 years later it seemed normal and relatively easy. That improvement was made in less than 25 years; if you go back another 50 years and imagine the state of orchestral playing in places like Brno then, you can see why people thought Janáček was mad or an amateur. There is no question that the technique of the average orchestral player has improved over the years. Another factor in solving the problems is the improvement in modern printing techniques. Scores and parts are now much more legible, with the music properly written out. If you saw the original parts for *Katya Kabanova* it is amazing that anyone was able to play it at all.

One problem which does remain is the question of Janáček's use of the viola d'amore. This is included in three orchestral works — *Katya Kabanova*, *The Makropulos Case*, and the Sinfonietta. Many Janáček scholars assumed that he did not really know what the instrument was like, and was simply attracted by its evocative name. (I actually feel the instrument's sympathetic strings give it a slightly unworldly character rather than one suggesting love.) But when I came to conduct these works for recordings I found that a lot of what he wrote for the viola d'amore was suitable for that instrument and not for the ordinary viola. It is unlikely that Janáček ever heard any of his works played with the viola d'amore but it would be wrong to assume that he did not know what it could do. There are passages in *The Makropulos Case* in which the viola d'amore is taken tremendously high — it is quite possible on that instrument because it has more strings and the top one is usually tuned to 'd', only a tone lower than a violin. The writing at the end of *The Makropulos Case* and in the third movement of the Sinfonietta, which is outrageous for an ordinary viola, is perfectly playable on the viola d'amore. The problem is that, without microphones, it is not possible to get the sound of the viola d'amore through the orchestra. So, when we recorded the Sinfonietta in Vienna, we used the viola d'amore but for the live performances at the same time we used ordinary violas. When I do any of these works in the future, if it is a practical possibility to mike up the viola d'amore I will have a try at it. It can be very tricky to have a microphone for one instrument only, especially in a crowded orchestra pit. The other problem is finding a player. We were lucky in Vienna because two members of the Vienna Philharmonic can play it, but it is not an instrument you can just pick up and play.

Sir Charles Mackerras was interviewed by John McMurray.

Kenneth Woollam as Boris and Ava June as Katya Kabanova at ENO (photo: Donald Southern)

Selective Discography

Cathy Peterson

Jenůfa

Conductor	*C. Mackerras*	*F. Jílek*
Orchestra/ Opera House	**Vienna PO**	**Brno Janáček Opera Orch.**
Date	*1977*	*1982*
Jenůfa	E. Söderström	G. Beňačková
Laca	W. Ochman	V. Přibyl
Števa	P. Dvorský	V. Krejík
Kostelnička	E. Randová	N. Kniplová
Mayor	D. Zitek	V. Halíř
Jano	J. Jonášová	J. Janská
UK Disc Number	SUP 2751/2	D276D3
UK Tape Number	—	K276K33
UK CD Number	—	414483-2
US Disc Number	SUP 2751/2	LDR73009
US Tape Number	—	—

Katya Kabanova

Conductor	*J. Krombholc*	*C. Mackerras*
Orchestra/ Opera House	**Prague National Theatre Orch.**	**Vienna PO**
Date	*1959*	*1976*
Dikoy	Z. Kroupa	D. Jedička
Boris	B. Blachut	P. Dvorský
Kudryash	V. Koči	Z. Švehia
Katya	D. Tikalová	E. Söderström
Kabanicha	L. Komancová	N. Kniplová
Varvara	I. Mixová	I. Márová
Kuligin	P. Jedlička	J. Souček
Tichon	B. Vick	V. Krečik
US Disc Number	50 781/2	D51D2
UK Tape Number	—	K51K22
US Disc Number	50 781/2	London 12109
US Tape Number	—	London 5-12109

Bibliography

The best biography of Janáček is Jaroslav Vogel's *Leoš Janáček: His Life and Works* (trans. K. Janovicky, London, 1981) but also available is *Leoš Janáček: His Life and Work* by H. Hollander (trans. P. Hamburger, London, 1963). *Jenůfa* and *Katya Kabanova* are discussed in *The Operas of Leoš Janáček* by E. Chisholm (Oxford, 1971) and *Janáček's Tragic Operas* by Mich—— ——s (London, 1977).

The Cambridge Opera ⌐
a detailed and scholar'
David Pountney
particular refere⌐

Janáček's ow⌐
selection is av⌐
Vilem and Marg⌐

Ostrovsky's *The Stoi.*
Wettlin, London, 1974).

Jaroslav Krejči is Professor Emeritus wo⌐
Lancaster; he taught mainly in the Depar⌐
published extensively on various social systems ⌐
Czechoslovakia, Poland, Yugoslavia and Austria, o⌐
social history. His most recent book is *Great Revol*⌐
Search for a Theory.

Karel Brusak is Visiting Lecturer in Czech and Slovak lit⌐
University of Cambridge. Apart from many articles on literature a⌐
of the semiotics of theatre and drama he has published a libretto for t⌐
act opera *The Utmost Sail* by Karel Janovický and several translations of ⌐
verse used in Janáček's choruses.

Arnold Whittall is Professor of Musical Theory and Analysis at King's College, University of London and has written widely on 19th and 20th century music, especially Wagner, Schoenberg, Britten and Tippett.

Jan Smaczny lectures in Music at Birmingham University. He writes on Czech music in general and Dvořák operas in particular.

Alex de Jonge is the author of several books about Russian literature and history. His biography of Joseph Stalin will be published in the Spring of 1986. He is a Fellow of New College, Oxford.

John Tyrrell is a Lecturer in Music at the University of Nottingham.

Sir Charles Mackerras was, from 1970-78, Music Director of Sadler's Wells/English National Opera and from 1987 will be Music Director of Welsh National Opera.

John McMurray is Publications Editor for The Royal Opera House, Covent Garden.

Bibliography

The best biography of Janáček is Jaroslav Vogel's *Leoš Janáček: His Life and Works* (trans. K. Janovicky, London, 1981) but also available is *Leoš Janáček: His Life and Work* by H. Hollander (trans. P. Hamburger, London, 1963). *Jenůfa* and *Katya Kabanova* are discussed in *The Operas of Leoš Janáček* by E. Chisholm (Oxford, 1971) and *Janáček's Tragic Operas* by Michael Ewans (London, 1977).

The Cambridge Opera Handbook, *Kát'a Kabanová* (ed. John Tyrrell, 1982) is a detailed and scholarly study of the opera and has an illuminating essay from David Pountney on the problems of producing Janáček operas, with particular reference to *Katya*.

Janáček's own prolific writings are largely unpublished in the UK, but a small selection is available in *Leoš Janáček: Leaves from his Life* (ed. and trans. by Vilem and Margaret Tausky, London, 1982).

Ostrovsky's *The Storm* is available in a collection of his plays (trans. M. Wettlin, London, 1974).

Contributors

Jaroslav Krejčí is Professor Emeritus working in research at the University of Lancaster; he taught mainly in the Department of European Studies and published extensively on various social systems in Germany (West and East), Czechoslovakia, Poland, Yugoslavia and Austria, on ethnic problems and on social history. His most recent book is *Great Revolutions Compared, the Search for a Theory*.

Karel Brusak is Visiting Lecturer in Czech and Slovak literature at the University of Cambridge. Apart from many articles on literature and studies of the semiotics of theatre and drama he has published a libretto for the one-act opera *The Utmost Sail* by Karel Janovický and several translations of folk verse used in Janáček's choruses.

Arnold Whittall is Professor of Musical Theory and Analysis at King's College, University of London and has written widely on 19th and 20th century music, especially Wagner, Schoenberg, Britten and Tippett.

Jan Smaczny lectures in Music at Birmingham University. He writes on Czech music in general and Dvořák operas in particular.

Alex de Jonge is the author of several books about Russian literature and history. His biography of Joseph Stalin will be published in the Spring of 1986. He is a Fellow of New College, Oxford.

John Tyrrell is a Lecturer in Music at the University of Nottingham.

Sir Charles Mackerras was, from 1970-78, Music Director of Sadler's Wells/English National Opera and from 1987 will be Music Director of Welsh National Opera.

John McMurray is Publications Editor for The Royal Opera House, Covent Garden.

Selective Discography

Cathy Peterson

Jenůfa

Conductor	C. Mackerras	F. Jílek
Orchestra/ Opera House	Vienna PO	Brno Janáček Opera Orch.
Date	1977	1982
Jenůfa	E. Söderström	G. Beňačková
Laca	W. Ochman	V. Přibyl
Števa	P. Dvorský	V. Krejík
Kostelnička	E. Randová	N. Kniplová
Mayor	D. Zítek	V. Halíř
Jano	J. Jonášová	J. Janská
UK Disc Number	SUP 2751/2	D276D3
UK Tape Number	—	K276K33
UK CD Number	—	414483-2
US Disc Number	SUP 2751/2	LDR73009
US Tape Number	—	—

Katya Kabanova

Conductor	J. Krombholc	C. Mackerras
Orchestra/ Opera House	Prague National Theatre Orch.	Vienna PO
Date	1959	1976
Dikoy	Z. Kroupa	D. Jedička
Boris	B. Blachut	P. Dvorský
Kudryash	V. Kočí	Z. Švehía
Katya	D. Tikalová	E. Söderström
Kabanicha	L. Komancová	N. Kniplová
Varvara	I. Mixová	I. Márová
Kuligin	P. Jedlička	J. Souček
Tichon	B. Vick	V. Krečík
US Disc Number	50 781/2	D51D2
UK Tape Number	—	K51K22
US Disc Number	50 781/2	London 12109
US Tape Number	—	London 5-12109